USDA

United States
Department
of Agriculture

Forest Service

Rocky Mountain
Research Station

General Technical Report
RMRS-GTR-236WWW

April 2010

Retrospective Fire Modeling:
Quantifying the Impacts of
Fire Suppression

I0447038

Brett H. Davis, Carol Miller, and Sean A. Parks

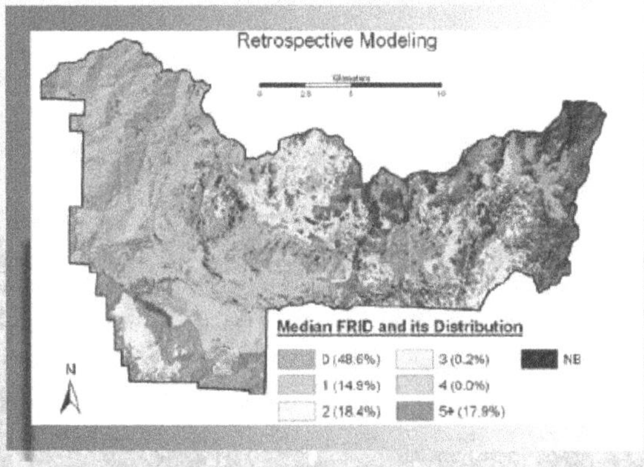

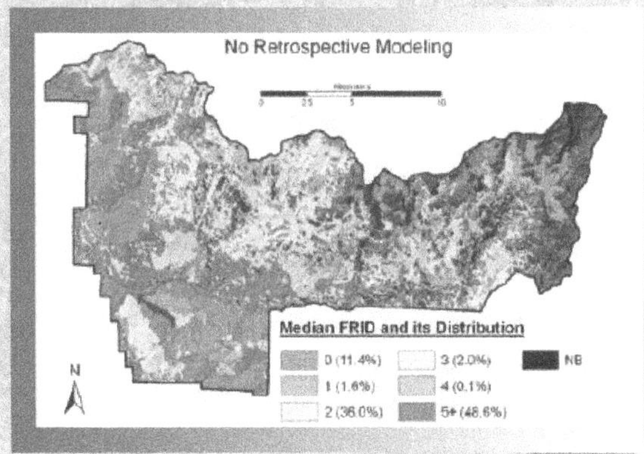

Davis, Brett H.; Miller, Carol; and Parks, Sean A. 2010. Retrospective fire modeling: Quantifying the impacts of fire suppression. Gen. Tech. Rep. RMRS-GTR-236WWW. Fort Collins, CO: U.S. Department of Agriculture, Forest Service, Rocky Mountain Research Station. 40 p.

Abstract

Land management agencies need to understand and monitor the consequences of their fire suppression decisions. We developed a framework for retrospective fire behavior modeling and impact assessment to determine where ignitions would have spread had they not been suppressed and to assess the cumulative effects that would have resulted. This document is a general guidebook for applying this methodology and is for land managers interested in quantifying the impacts of fire suppression. Using this methodology will help land managers track the cumulative effects of suppression, frame future suppression decisions and cost-benefit analyses in the context of past experiences, and communicate tradeoffs to the public, non-government organizations, land management agencies, and other interested parties.

Keywords: fire behavior prediction, fire effects, fire modeling, retrospective, impact assessment

Authors

Brett Davis is a GIS Specialist and Fire Modeler with the Aldo Leopold Wilderness Research Institute, Rocky Mountain Research Station, USDA Forest Service. His professional interests include GIS analysis and automation, fire modeling, wildland fire use, and the relationship between wilderness health and wildland fire. Brett received his M.S. degree in Forestry (with an emphasis on GIS, remote sensing and fire) from Colorado State University and his B.A. degree in Biology and Psychology from the University of Colorado at Boulder.

Dr. Carol Miller is a Research Ecologist with RMRS, Aldo Leopold Wilderness Research Institute. Her research seeks to develop the knowledge necessary to improve the stewardship of fire as a natural process in wilderness and similarly protected lands.

Sean Parks is a GIS Specialist with the Aldo Leopold Wilderness Research Institute. He received a B.S. degree in Environmental Biology and an M.A. degree in Geography, both from University of California, Davis.

You may order additional copies of this publication by sending your mailing information in label form through one of the following media. Please specify the publication title and series number.

Fort Collins Service Center

Telephone	(970) 498-1392
FAX	(970) 498-1122
E-mail	rschneider@fs.fed.us
Web site	http://www.fs.fed.us/rm/publications
Mailing address	Publications Distribution
	Rocky Mountain Research Station
	240 West Prospect Road
	Fort Collins, CO 80526

Rocky Mountain Research Station
240 W. Prospect Road
Fort Collins, Colorado 80526

Contents

Acknowledgments

This project was supported by the Joint Fire Science Program and the Rocky Mountain Research Station. The authors would like to thank the following people for their invaluable contributions to this project: Dave Bartlett, Mike Beasley, Jen Beck, Tony Caprio, Corky Conover, Karen Folger, Andi Thode, Jan van Wagtendonk, and Kent van Wagtendonk. We would also like to thank our reviewers Tobin Kelley and Kent van Wagtendonk. Laurie Kurth and Chuck McHugh's invaluable comments led to an improved revision.

Introduction

When wildfires are suppressed, opportunities are foregone to create fuel breaks, reduce fire regime departures, and decrease future extreme fire behavior by modifying fuels. To our knowledge, no one has yet attempted to systematically quantify these foregone opportunities. This general technical report describes a methodology to measure the cumulative impacts of suppression over time by modeling the spread of ignitions that were suppressed. We illustrate a set of analysis steps to simulate where ignitions would have spread had they not been suppressed and to assess the cumulative effects that would have resulted from those fires. The quantification of these effects will help land managers improve the prioritization and planning of fuels treatments and help inform decisions about the suppression of future ignitions.

In its simplest application, the methodology compares two landscapes: the realized landscape vs. a hypothetical landscape. As used throughout this guidebook, a "landscape" refers mainly to the biophysical characteristics of the study area such as vegetation and fuel conditions and potential fire behavior. The realized landscape is the landscape that resulted due to the fire management strategies actually implemented; this is typically the current landscape. The hypothetical landscape is the landscape that would have resulted if different fire management strategies had been chosen (e.g., if one or more suppressed ignitions had been allowed to burn freely). While the examples in this guidebook compare only two landscapes, any number of landscapes could be compared. A case study examines what conditions might have resulted if lightning-ignited fires were not suppressed in the South Fork Merced watershed of Yosemite National Park.

The retrospective modeling process requires modeling the spread of ignitions that were suppressed, updating the fuels data to reflect that modeled fire, and repeating this process to account for all the ignitions of interest throughout the simulation period; this results in the hypothetical landscape. Once the modeling cycles are complete, the final step involves assessing the impacts of fire suppression by comparing the hypothetical and realized landscapes using various metrics depending on need and purpose. For example, the hypothetical and realized landscapes might be compared in terms of potential fire behavior (i.e., flame length or crowning potential).

This document is a guidebook in that it provides a moderate level of detail for implementing the methodology and uses a case study to illustrate some procedures. However, it does not provide step-by-step instructions. Furthermore, inputs and parameters used in the case study are for illustration and should not be applied uncritically to other situations. Occasionally, specific tips on how best to accomplish the required steps are offered, but this guidebook is not intended to be a tutorial for specific modeling software, nor is it a text on fire behavior, ecology, or management.

To implement the methodology here, the user must have some basic skill sets. The most important skills include basic Geographic Information System (GIS) data manipulation and analysis, experience with fire growth modeling software such as FARSITE (Finney 1998), and familiarity with fire management terminology. Other useful skills include familiarity with other fire modeling software such as FlamMap (Finney 2006) and FireFamilyPlus (FFP; Bradshaw and McCormick 2000), and knowledge of fuels characterization, fire weather analysis, fire behavior, fire ecology, and fire management.

The first section of this guidebook describes how to set up the project, followed by a section that explains how to conduct the data preparation, modeling and analysis. Below is a checklist of steps recommended to implement a retrospective fire modeling analysis and impact assessment.

Setting Up the Project

Define Project Goals

First and foremost, it is important to define the reasons for running a retrospective fire modeling analysis and how the impacts of suppression are going to be measured. The purpose of a retrospective analysis is to answer "what if" questions. For example, what if a particular set of ignitions had been allowed to burn? How would those fires have affected fuel loading, landscape condition, and potential fire behavior? Fire suppression impacts can be measured by comparing the resulting hypothetical and realized landscape conditions. Impacts of suppression might be measured in terms of fire regime departure, potential fire behavior, future ignition occurrence, and/or smoke emissions.

Define Project Parameters

Next, a few broad project parameters must be defined. These include defining the study area (park, forest, watershed, etc.). Second, determining the time span of interest (e.g., 11 years from 1994-2004), taking into consideration the availability of quality input data, computer processing capabilities, and the amount of time available to perform the analysis. The third step is defining the length of the fire season. These general parameters can be determined by consulting with local fire managers such as the Fire Management Officer (FMO) or by analyzing historical fire weather and fire occurrence data. A final consideration is that all spatial data must have a common projection, cell size, and extent.

EXAMPLE

Project parameters

Study area: South Fork Merced watershed, Yosemite National Park
Simulation length: 11 years, 1994-2004
Fire season definition: June-October
Spatial data properties: UTM projection; 90 m cell size

Choose Metric(s) to Quantify and Compare Alternative Landscapes

As previously mentioned, quantifiable metrics are needed to assess the impacts of differing fire management strategies. Below are some suggested metrics. Other metrics may be developed and used depending on the goals of the project, geographic location, and personal preference.

Fire Regime Departure

Measures of fire regime departure compare the frequency of fire in the distant past (typically pre-European "settlement") to the frequency of fire in the recent past (since effective fire suppression began). They are used to gauge the deviation of current fire patterns from historical norms.

Fire Return Interval Departure (FRID): FRID data are developed by determining how many years have passed since an area last burned and dividing that number by the characteristic Fire Return Interval (FRI) of the underlying vegetation. FRI represents a time interval between successive fire events. It is used to gauge how often a particular vegetation type would burn under natural conditions. FRI is based on fire history studies and stratified by vegetation types. For example, the mean FRI for giant sequoia forests has been calculated to be 10 years (Caprio and Lineback 2002). FRID, on the other hand, represents the number of FRIs that have been missed at a particular location. Therefore, a giant sequoia forest that has not experienced a fire for 50 years has a Fire Return Interval Departure of 5 (50 divided by 10 = 5).

Fire Regime Condition Class (FRCC): FRCC is a standardized metric for determining the degree of departure from reference condition vegetation, fuels, and disturbance regimes (Schmidt and others 2002). FRCC is divided into three departure classes: low, moderate, and high. A low departure represents areas within their natural range of variability (*sensu* Landres and others 1999) while moderate and high departures describe areas outside their natural range of variability.

In the case study, FRID is used instead of FRCC, because it is considered a finer measure of departure from natural conditions and because the fire managers in the case study area prefer this metric. They use it to estimate the degree to which an area's vegetation has been modified relative to the vegetation and structure that may have occurred had fires been allowed to burn naturally (Caprio and others 2002).

Fire Behavior

A number of fire behavior characteristics can be used to measure the impacts of suppression.

Crown fire occurrence: Categorical measure predicting whether a fire is a surface fire, passive crown fire (torching), or an active crown fire.

Fireline intensity: The rate of heat energy released per unit length of flaming fire front. Fireline intensity is usually expressed in BTU/s/ft or kW/m.

Flame length: Distance from the tip of the flame to the middle of the flaming zone at the base of the fire. Flame length is measured on an angle when wind and/or slope are tilting the flame.

Rate of spread: The relative activity of a fire in extending its horizontal dimensions. Depending on the intended use of the information, rate of spread can be expressed as the rate of increase of the total perimeter of the fire, as the rate of forward spread of the fire front, or as the rate of increase in area.

In the case study, flame length is used, because it is a good indicator of fire intensity. Flame length can also be used as a proxy for firefighter safety and to determine attack strategies (National Interagency Fire Center 2006).

Smoke Emissions

Smoke emissions contain a variety of gases and particulate matter. PM 2.5 (Particulate Matter smaller than 2.5 microns) and PM 10 emissions are the most commonly tracked components of wildfire smoke because of their potential impacts on human health. Simulated smoke emissions can be quantified on a per-fire modeling year basis and totaled at the end of the last simulation year in the retrospective analysis. Alternatively, *potential* smoke emissions—the emissions that would result if the entire landscape burned—can be estimated and used to compare landscapes created by alternative management strategies.

Model Selection

Any model is merely an attempt to represent reality and will never be completely accurate. George Box (1979) put it well when he said, "All models are wrong, but some are useful." The methodology described in this guidebook is no exception. It is subject to all the underlying assumptions and limitations of the different models used. It is the responsibility of users to familiarize themselves with these assumptions and limitations to ensure the correct interpretation of the results.

There are many models needed to effectively carry out a retrospective fire modeling analysis. A weather analysis tool is required to create the weather information necessary to model fires and to determine fire-ending weather events. A fire growth model is used to predict the spread and final perimeter of each ignition. A fuel succession model is necessary to update the fuels layer(s) after a fire. A fire behavior model is used to compare the hypothetical and realized landscapes. Finally, a smoke emissions model can be used to compare potential emissions on hypothetical and realized landscapes. This guide focuses on the models used in the case study. However, alternative models are sometimes suggested, and users may choose any model they deem appropriate. General guidance on many of the following models can be found in *Guidance on Spatial Wildland Fire Analysis: Models, Tools and Techniques* (Stratton 2006), available at http://www.fs.fed.us/rm/pubs/rmrs_gtr183.pdf.

Weather Analysis

Historical weather data need to be reviewed, analyzed, and manipulated for use in the fire growth and fire behavior models and to determine fire-ending weather events, such as significant precipitation. This process may be as simple as extracting input weather and wind data for use in a fire growth simulation model, or more complex, such as analyzing historical fire weather patterns to aid in the selection of historical ignitions. FireFamilyPlus (FFP), a fire climatology and occurrence analysis program, is well suited to perform either of these tasks. FFP can be used in retrospective fire modeling to define fire seasons, calculate fire weather index percentiles, calculate daily values of relevant weather indices, identify significant precipitation events, and export required weather and wind inputs for a fire growth or behavior model. Its calculations can be used to help select which ignitions to model and at what times they might be expected to spread. Many of these functions could also be performed using spreadsheet and/or text editing programs, but a program like FFP greatly simplifies the task.

Fire Growth

A fire growth model is the heart of the retrospective fire modeling process and is needed to predict the spread and final perimeter of each ignition. FARSITE is the most commonly used decision support system in the United States for modeling fire growth. It uses spatial information on topography and fuels, along with weather and wind data, to simulate the spread and behavior of wildland fires (Finney 1998). FARSITE is actually an assemblage of several underlying models including surface fire spread (Albini 1976, Rothermel 1972), spotting

(Albini 1979), crown fire spread (Rothermel 1991, Van Wagner 1977, 1993), fuel moisture dynamics (Nelson 2000), and others. As such, all the assumptions and limitations of these models apply to FARSITE as well. In addition to fire growth modeling, FARSITE can be used to model fire behavior (e.g., flame length) and smoke production. Its spatial input data layers are organized into a single "landscape" (LCP) file, which can also be used as an input to the fire behavior modeling tool FlamMap. Throughout the remainder of this guide, FARSITE and FlamMap's landscape files will be referred to as LCP files to reduce confusion with the hypothetical and realized landscapes. LCP files require spatial data describing surface fuel models, topography, and canopy cover. Optional LCP file data include stand height, crown base height, crown bulk density, duff loading, and coarse woody debris. These optional inputs are necessary for crown fire and/or emissions modeling. FARSITE has been widely used for projections of active wildfire spread and behavior and for planning purposes. It is particularly well suited for asking multiple "what if" questions and comparing the results. FARSITE was used as the fire growth model in the case study. One alternative to FARSITE is the Canadian wildland fire growth model Prometheus (Tymstra and others 2009).

Fuel Succession

A fuel succession model is necessary to update the fuels layer(s) after each fire. Fuel loadings will change through time with disturbance and vegetative accumulation. Multi-year retrospective fire modeling requires that fuel data be updated to reflect these dynamics. After each fire, fuels data must be updated to account for the changes caused by the fire; similarly, if the time span of a project is long enough for fuel accumulation to occur, fuels data must be updated to account for those changes as well. Therefore, it is necessary to model fuel succession.

For the case study, an expert-opinion based fuel succession model was developed in collaboration with scientists and managers from Yosemite and Sequoia-Kings Canyon National Parks and the United States Geological Survey (USGS) for use in the Sierra Nevada (Davis and others 2009). This model was used for the case study, but a number of existing models could be used alone, or in conjunction with each other, to obtain similar results. For example, FOFEM (First Order Fire Effects Model; Reinhardt and others 1997), FVS-FFE (Forest Vegetation Simulator—Fire and Fuels Extension; Reinhardt and Crookston 2003), and/or simplistic crosswalks based on local/expert opinion. Local experts should be consulted whether a new fuel succession model is created or existing models are used.

The fuel succession model used in the case study is a state and transition model describing transitions between fire behavior fuel models (Scott and Burgan 2005). It is represented by diagrams of succession describing fuel accumulation and disturbance by fire (Fig. 1) and predicts fuel model transitions in both the absence of fire and after a fire of a particular severity. These transitions are based on estimated fuel accumulation rates and how the underlying vegetation would be expected to respond after fires of different severities.

To illustrate how this fuel succession model operates, consider a Timber Litter 3 (TL3; moderate load conifer litter) fuel model (Fig. 1). If an area of TL3 fuels experiences a low severity fire, it temporarily transitions to an unburnable state and then back to a TL3 model after a 20-year recovery (i.e., fuel accumulation)

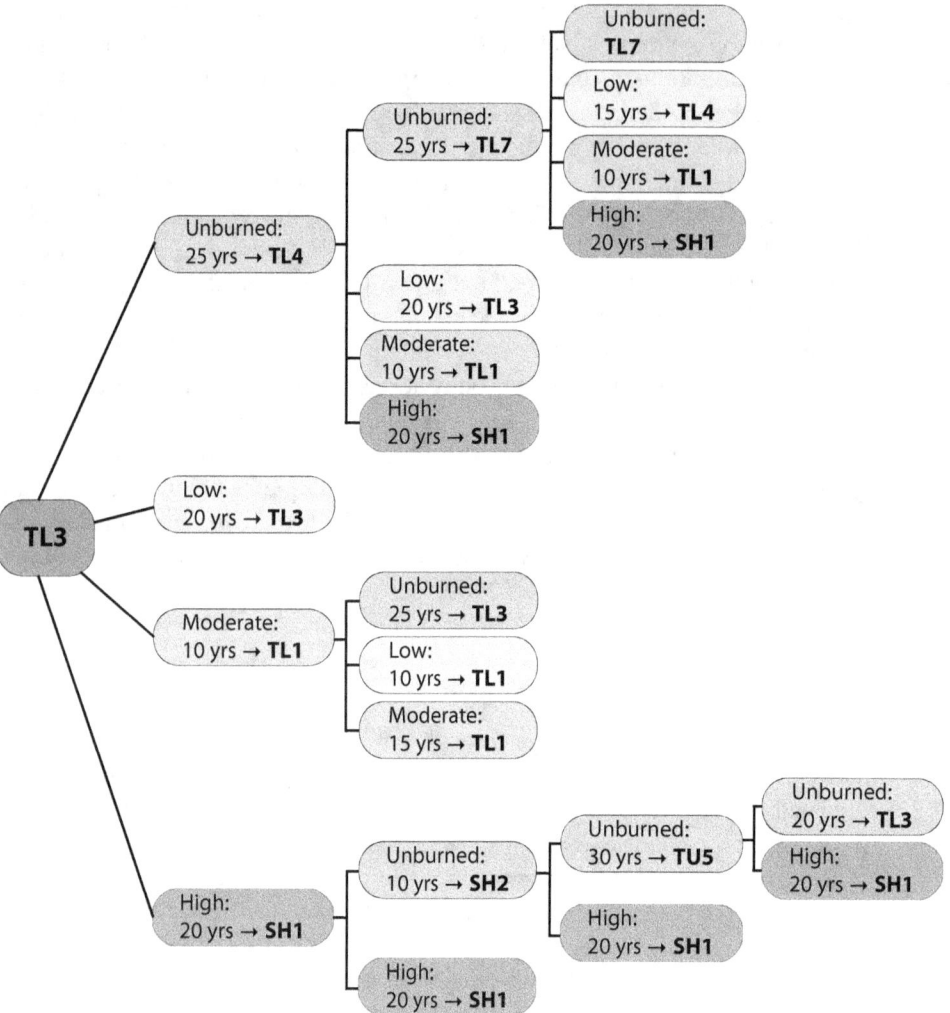

Figure 1. Fuel succession diagram for moderate load of conifer litter (TL3). SH = shrub.

period. After a moderate severity fire, TL3 transitions to unburnable, then to a Timber Litter 1 (TL1; low load compact conifer litter) fuel model after 10 years. After a high severity fire, it transitions to unburnable, then to a Shrub 1 (SH1; low load dry climate shrub) fuel model after 20 years. Finally, if it remains unburned for 25 years, it transitions to a Timber Litter 4 (TL4; small downed logs) model. During the recovery period (i.e., the time between the fire and the transition when the area is in an "unburnable" state), the burned area is considered to have too little fuel to carry another fire. The fuel models and transition times were selected based on the characteristics of the underlying vegetation.

For more detailed information on how this fuel succession model works see Davis and others (2009).

Fire Behavior

To compare the hypothetical and realized landscapes with each other, it is useful to estimate the potential fire behavior for the entire landscape given a set of static environmental conditions. Although the fire growth simulator FARSITE can be used to predict fire behavior, it does so only within the perimeter of each modeled fire, not the entire landscape. In the case study, the spatial fire behavior modeling tool FlamMap was used for this purpose. FlamMap requires an

LCP file, fuel moisture and wind data (Finney 2006). FlamMap can calculate independent potential fire behavior for each pixel on a landscape for a single point-in-time. FlamMap predicts numerous fire behavior characteristics (e.g., flame length, rate of spread, crowning index) that can be used to compare the hypothetical and realized landscapes. BehavePlus (Andrews and others 2005) is another tool that potentially could be used to make comparative fire behavior and risk predictions.

Smoke Emissions

A smoke emissions model can be used to compare emissions from the hypothetical and realized landscapes. Emissions can be estimated for each simulation year during the process and compiled at the end of the last simulation year. Additionally, estimating an entire landscape's potential emissions, based on estimating the potential emissions from all burnable pixels, can provide useful comparative information. In the case study, this comparative application was used to estimate emissions for the final landscapes resulting from both the hypothetical and realized scenarios. The case study used the GIS-based Emissions Estimation System (EES) (Clinton and others 2003) to quantify wildland fire emissions. EES uses FOFEM fuel consumption and emission estimation algorithms in a spatially explicit manner. It can be used in retrospective fire modeling to calculate PM 2.5 and PM 10 emissions for any modeled fire's final perimeter. In addition, it can be used to predict potential emissions, as described above, for entire landscapes. Currently, EES only contains data for modeling emissions in California, but it could potentially be adapted to work in other areas. Alternative tools for estimating emissions include FARSITE and FOFEM. FARSITE can be used to estimate emissions during the fire growth modeling process, provided the user has the necessary duff and coarse woody debris data.

Data Acquisition and Preparation

Project parameters (study area location, simulation time span, and length of fire season) will dictate what and how much data are necessary. The basic data required for a retrospective fire-modeling project include:

- Boundary delineating the study area
- Historical ignition point location and timing within the study area
- Historical weather data from Remote Automated Weather Stations (RAWS) or similar weather stations covering the simulation period. Hourly data are preferable but where they are unavailable, daily data can be supplemented.
- Surface and canopy fuels data that reflect conditions at the beginning of the simulation period as nearly as possible
- Topographic data (elevation, slope, and aspect)
- Digital fire atlas data (polygons)
- Optional: Fire severity data for real fires that occurred during the simulation period
- Optional: Fire Return Interval (FRI) data if FRID is chosen as an impact measure
- Optional: Spatial duff and coarse woody debris data if emissions are being modeled using FARSITE

- Other data may be required depending on the models, outputs, and methodologies selected.

TIP

Data Acquisition

If possible, attempt to obtain data that extends beyond the study area to reduce edge effects.

Each of these datasets is described below with suggestions on where to acquire them.

Study Area Boundary

The study area boundary (Fig. 2) should be obtained from local management staff and typically needs no particular manipulation other than to ensure that it is in the desired geographic projection. This boundary is used to define the analysis area and to manipulate (e.g., clip) ignition and fuels data layers.

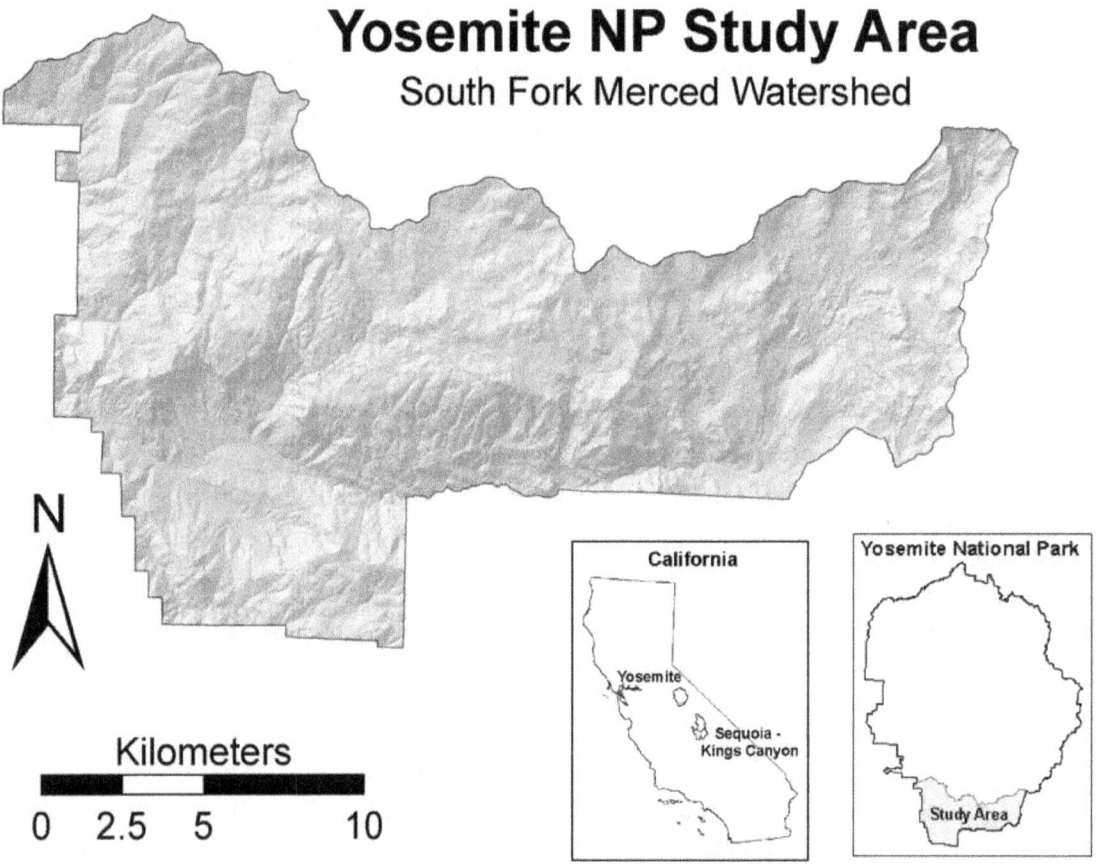

Figure 2. South Fork Merced study area, Yosemite NP.

Historical Weather Data

Successful retrospective fire modeling depends on high quality weather information. Weather data are very important inputs for fire growth and behavior modeling. Inaccurate or incomplete weather data will lead to inaccurate fire growth and behavior predictions. Time and effort spent on acquiring and preparing these data will ultimately pay off in increased confidence in the outputs.

Acquiring historical weather data: Remote Automated Weather Station (RAWS) data are the most commonly used weather data in the United States for fire modeling. When possible, hourly, rather than daily, weather data should be used. Some hourly (.fw9 format) and daily (.fwx format) RAWS data for the entire United States can be acquired from the Western Regional Climate Center (WRCC) website (http://www.wrcc.dri.edu/fpa/). FFP requires the weather data itself (.fwx or .fw9) and a station catalog file (.txt). Catalog files are available from the National Wildfire Coordinating Group's (NWCG) website (http://fam. nwcg.gov/fam-web/) under the "Fire and Weather data" link (FFP 4.02 has catalog information pre-loaded for most RAWS stations). Information should be verified that it is up-to-date as there are often delays in archiving these data. Daily RAWS data (but not hourly) can also be acquired from NWCG's website. Information about RAWS and other types of weather stations (including locations) can be found at http://www.raws.dri.edu/index.html.

Selecting a weather station should be done in consultation with a local expert with fire management and modeling experience. To be representative of the study area as a whole, the station should be as near the average elevation and the center of the study area as possible. Another consideration is the influence of surrounding topography on wind direction and speed. Wind direction and speed should be as representative of the whole study area as possible and not overly influenced by topography (e.g., being in a wind shadow). If necessary, more than one weather station might better represent conditions in the study area. For example, one may be used for weather data (precipitation, temperature, humidity) and another for wind (speed and azimuth). Wind rose plots are helpful for evaluating the representativeness of weather stations.

The station(s) selected should also have complete and accurate records. RAWS data are particularly prone to missing and erroneous data. The longer the time period covered, the more likely these data will contain errors. FFP can be used to locate erroneous and missing data (see "Preparing weather data" below). There should be no large gaps in the hourly/daily records for the months of the fire season. Although finding stations that fit all these strict requirements may be difficult, it is important to adhere to them as closely as possible. Once the station(s) have been selected, download the weather (*.fwx or *.fw9) and catalog files (*.txt) if necessary.

EXAMPLE

Weather Station Selection

Weather data: Mariposa Grove RAWS (#44113), good hourly data but in a sheltered location

Wind data: Metcalf Gap RAWS (#44209), outside of the study area but in an unsheltered location on a ridge west of the study area

Both chosen in consultation with an experienced FARSITE user at Yosemite National Park

---

Preparing weather data: Much of the weather data analysis described in this guidebook requires the use of FireFamilyPlus (FFP). If a program other than FFP is being used to analyze and prepare the weather data, the general concepts described below can be followed to replicate the analysis. Preparing weather data requires several steps: importing and reviewing for missing data and errors, calculating a threshold value for fire growth (optional), calculating daily values for critical variables, and creating weather and wind streams for use in fire growth and behavior models.

Importing and reviewing weather station data: The first step is to import the weather and catalog files into FFP. If these files were downloaded from different sources, it may be necessary to reconcile the station IDs so they will be correctly associated in FFP.

TIP

Reviewing Weather Data

Look at FFP's import error log for information on erroneous values. Inspect the imported data by listing weather observations in FFP (Weather > View Observations > All). Sort the resultant table by each weather variable to look for erroneous or missing data. Obvious data errors will need to be removed or replaced with average values, previous values, values from another nearby weather station, etc. The number of records reviewed can be reduced by setting the "Data Years" and "Time of Year" filters before viewing "all observations." They can be reduced further if the first ignition selected for modeling in a particular year occurs substantially after the beginning of the fire season (see the "Preparing ignition data" section below).

It may be necessary to carry out more detailed quality control measures. For periods outside of the fire spread modeling dates (used for fire weather index calculations, etc.), a few errors can probably be ignored if the dataset is large enough. But, for those days when fire spread will actually be modeled, it is important to have weather data that are complete and as accurate as possible. This can be accomplished by editing the data within FFP or by importing the historical weather file into a spreadsheet program, such as Microsoft Excel, which facilitates the replacement of missing and erroneous data with averages or previous data. Unfortunately, the data cannot be saved back into a fw* format from Excel and therefore will need to be saved as one of the various text formats and manipulated with a text editor to return it to its original fw* format. Format details can be found at http://fam.nwcg.gov/fam-web/.

Calculating fire weather index percentiles (optional): At the discretion of the user, modeled fire growth can be limited to the days and times of day when fire is most likely to have substantial spread. This approach is highly recommended for use with FARSITE to reign in its propensity to over predict fire spread and to vastly shorten the time it takes to run a simulation (see "Modeling Fire Growth and Behavior" section below). A daily "burn period" is often used in FARSITE simulations to pause the simulation during periods of low fire activity, such as on cool nights when relative humidity increases. Historical fire spread can be used to identify conditions under which significant fire growth is likely. A "spread threshold" can be defined in terms of a fire weather index such as Energy Release Component (ERC) or Spread Component (SC), or fuel moisture. For example, if analysis of historical fires showed significant fire growth when ERC values exceeded 45, fire growth would only be simulated on days when the ERC ≥ 45. This threshold can also be expressed in terms of a percentile (e.g., 90th percentile ERC). Spread thresholds can also be used to adjust the length of the burning period. For example, when a fire index is extremely high, fires might grow significantly during the night and the burning period may need to be increased.

EXAMPLE

Setting Fire Growth Thresholds

In the case study, historical fire spread was not analyzed to determine thresholds. Insead, local managers defined the spread threshold as the 90th percentile ERC for the 1994-2004 seasons. While fire may spread at lower ERCs, the majority of spread occurs under extreme conditions. Setting the threshold greatly reduced modeling time. In addition, the daily burning period was increased from 9 hours (0900-1800) to 24 hours if ERC crossed the 98th percentile threshold, again based on local knowledge.

TIP

Calculating ERC

When using ERC to define a threshold for fire growth, the weather record should be buffered by approximately 40 days prior to the start of the season to ensure proper calculation of the 1000-hour fuel moistures, which are an important component for calculating ERC.

Set FFP's "Annual Filter" to the length of the fire season (e.g., June-October; Fig. 3) including as many years of high-quality data as are available but taking care to avoid climate trends that may be unrepresentative (e.g., Heinsch et al. 2009). Daily weather data (.fwx) are used to calculate these percentiles.

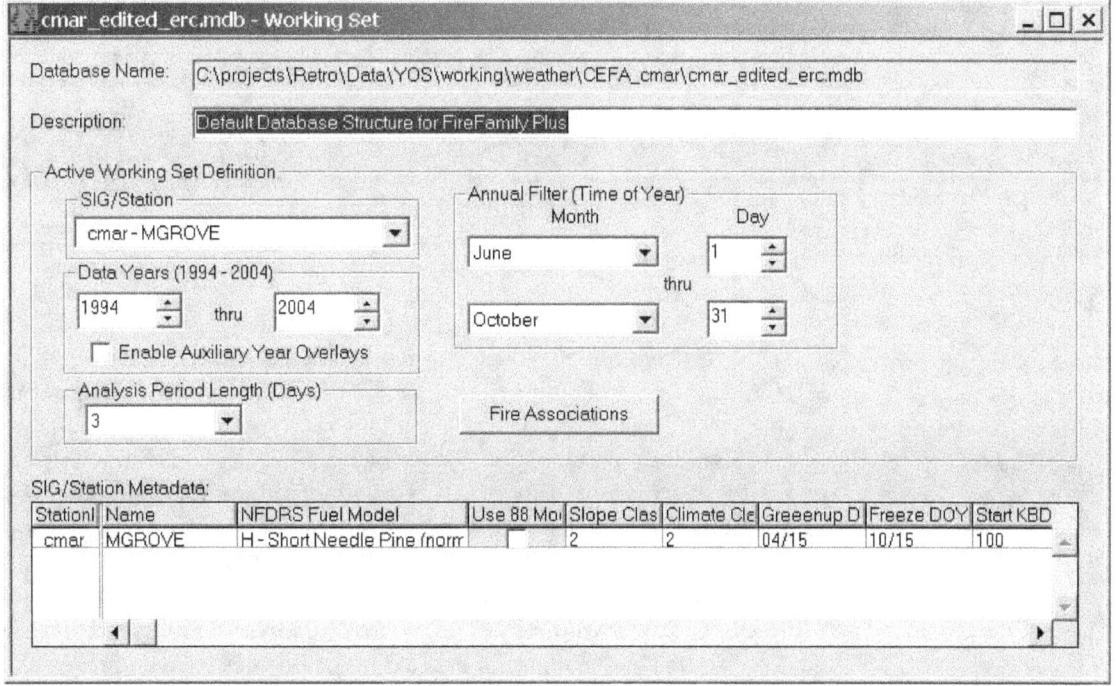

Figure 3. FFP "Working Set" screen.

The threshold value of the 90th percentile ERC used in the case study equates to an ERC value of 45 (Fig. 4). If a different dataset is used to calculate the fire weather index percentile than the dataset used to define the fire growth weather variables, be sure to switch back to the correct dataset before proceeding with the next step.

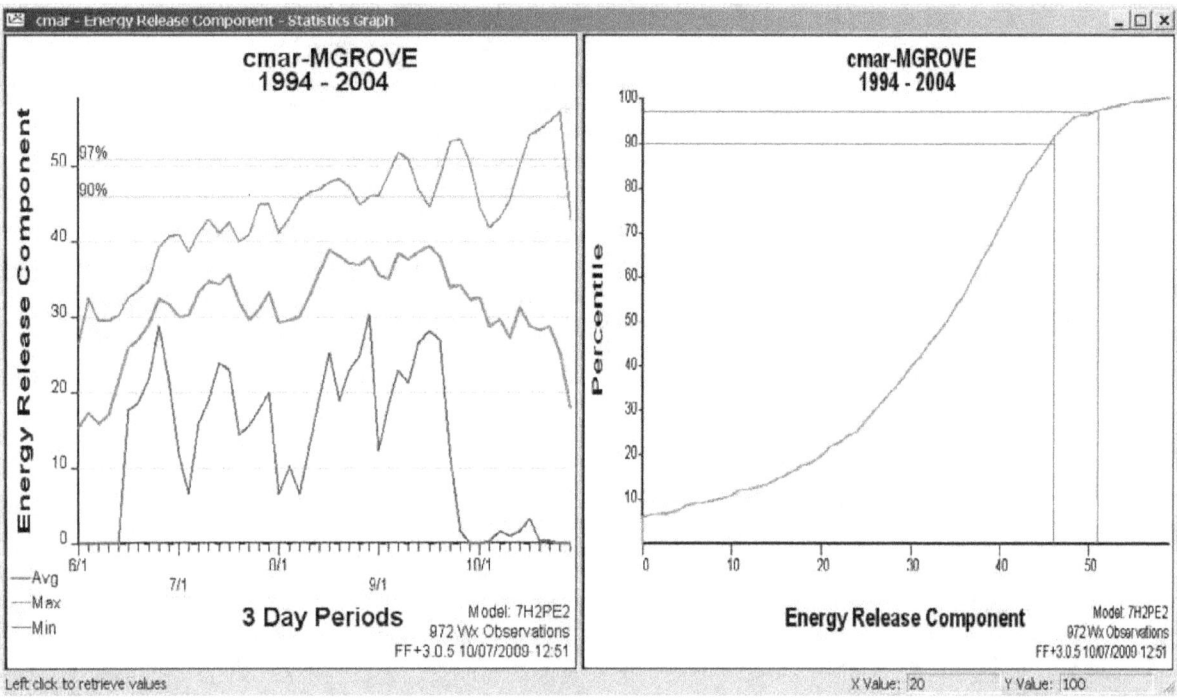

Figure 4. FFP percentile ERC graphs.

Calculating fire-ending events: Next, it is necessary to define and identify fire-ending events. For the case study a fire-ending event in the Yosemite area was defined as 0.5 inches of rain within a three-day period. Significant precipitation events such as this can be identified using FFP's "Event Locator" (Fig. 5). The exact definition of a fire-ending precipitation event will depend on the geographic area and fuel type and should be defined by a local fire behavior expert. Precipitation events that fall below the level judged capable of extinguishing a fire are commonly referred to as fire slowing events. The slowing effect these events have will be reflected by the impact increased fuel moistures have on fire growth modeling. They can be further accounted for when a fire weather index is used as a spread threshold.

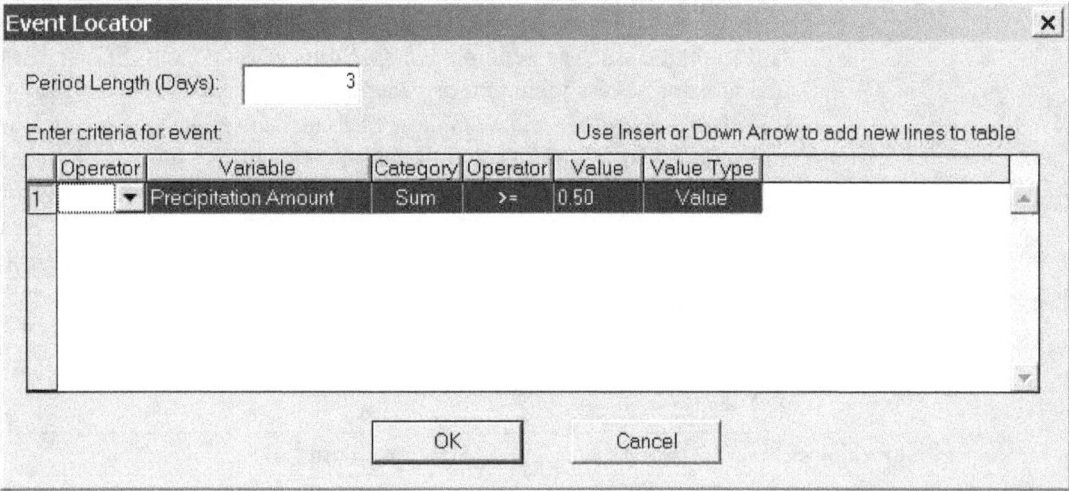

Figure 5. FFP's Event Locator.

EXAMPLE

Identifying Fire-Ending Events

1) Set "Data Years" on FFP's "Working Set" screen to the length of the simulation (e.g., 1994-2004).
2) Set "Annual Filter" to the length of the fire season (e.g., June 1-October 31).
3) Use Weather > Event Locator, input the appropriate values for the fire ending event (fig. 5).
4) Save or print the results for future reference.

Creating a list of relevant daily weather values: To help determine the exact dates for which fire growth will be simulated, it helps to have a list of those daily weather values that can affect the simulation. Relevant weather attributes include any index for which a threshold has been defined and any other variables of interest (e.g., precipitation, spread component). While it is more convenient to define a set date for the end of the fire season when analyzing historical data and calculating fire weather index percentiles, there are other options which may be more appropriate for the years in which fire spread will be modeled. For example, the end of the fire season is commonly defined as the point at which ERC falls below a certain level and doesn't recover. No matter how the end of the fire season is determined, a "pre-fire season" buffer of weather records will allow for a more accurate calculation of 1000-hr fuel moisture and therefore an index like ERC.

EXAMPLE

Generating a Daily Listing of Weather Values in FFP

This list can be developed by using FFP's Weather > Season Reports > Daily Listing, selecting the appropriate variables and saving the result as a text file for future reference.

DATE	ERC	SC	RAIN	1000 hr FM		DATE	ERC	SC	RAIN	1000 hr FM
19940601	29	9	0.00	20		19941025	45	10	0.00	8
19940602	31	12	0.00	19		19941026	46	10	0.00	8
19940603	33	10	0.00	19		19941027	46	11	0.00	8
19940604	30	10	0.00	19		19941028	48	13	0.00	7
19940605	29	9	0.00	18		19941029	12	2	0.40	9
. . .						19941030	8	1	0.20	9
						19941031	1	1	0.10	9

In the example above, ERC is used as the threshold index for fire growth and rain amount defines fire-ending events. Spread Component (SC) and 1000-hour fuel moistures were included for general interest.

Preparing weather and wind files: FFP can be used to generate weather (.wtr) and wind (.wnd) input files and to determine dead fuel moistures for the beginning of each fire season. Although FFP can generate live woody and herbaceous fuel moistures, it is recommended that live fuel moistures be determined in some other way (L. Kurth, USDA Forest Service, Rocky Mountain Research Station, personal communication). One weather file, one wind file, and at least one set of fuel moistures are required for each simulation year. As FARSITE does not change live fuel moistures with time, more than one set of moistures may be necessary to reflect seasonal changes.

EXAMPLE

To generate weather and wind files from hourly data in FFP, set the "Data Years" and "Time of Year" filters to the appropriate durations. Then use Weather > Hourly Data Analysis > FarSite Exports to generate the files. Repeat for each simulation year. To generate dead fuel moisture for input into FARSITE, calculate the 1-h, 10-h, and 100-h fuel moistures for the day of each year's first ignition with Weather > Season Reports > Daily Listing, selecting the appropriate variables (fuel moistures) and making a note of the values for the appropriate days.

TIP

Generating FARSITE Inputs

FARSITE inputs are not needed for the entire fire season if there are time periods when fire growth won't be simulated. Days can be excluded, for example, if the first ignition doesn't occur until a month into the fire season or if a fire-ending event occurs before the end of the fire season.

If FARSITE is used, fuel moisture files (.fms) for each year are necessary. Follow FARSITE's help file to correctly format these files.

The preceding steps should yield the following weather information:

1. Daily weather values for each fire season (e.g., *.wtr file)

2. Hourly (or daily) wind values for each year's season (e.g., *.wnd file)

3. Starting fuel moistures (1-h, 10-h, 100-h Live Herbaceous, and Live Woody) for the first day of each fire season or the first day of the simulation. (e.g., values used to create, with a text editor, the *.fms file)

4. Daily listing of fire weather index values, rain amounts and other values of interest

5. List of fire-ending (precipitation) events

Historical Ignition Data

Ignition data (location and date) should be as spatially and temporally accurate as possible. Dates and locations of suppressed ignitions help determine whether or not the ignition would have become an established wildfire, and hence need to be modeled. Cause, final fire size, and management response are also highly relevant pieces of information.

Acquiring ignition data: Historical ignition data for USDA Forest Service land reside in the National Interagency Fire Management Integrated Database (NIFMID). Historical ignition data for the Department of the Interior lands (NPS, BLM, FWS and BIA) reside in the Wildland Fire Management Information system (WFMI). Ignition data from both of these databases can be obtained from the National Wildfire Coordinating Group's (NWCG) website (http://fam.nwcg.gov/fam-web/ under "Fire and Weather data" link on the left).

These data have numerous, well-documented shortcomings, many of which are outlined in the Program for Climate, Ecosystem and Fire Application's (CEFA) "Coarse Assessment of Federal Wildland Fire Occurrence Data" (Brown and others 2002; http://www.cefa.dri.edu/Publications/fireoccurrencereport.pdf). In addition to this report, CEFA has developed a database of federal ignition points in which some of the grossest errors have been corrected or flagged. To obtain these data, use the contacts listed in the CEFA report. Another potential source for these data may be the land management agencies themselves who may have performed some quality control on their historical ignition data.

Preparing ignition data: Ignition location and attribute data (e.g., start date, cause, management response, and final fire size) are necessary to determine which ignitions were suppressed and whether they had the potential for significant growth. Ignitions of interest may be defined by attributes (e.g., lightning-caused), location, timing or any other selection criteria deemed important.

EXAMPLE

Initial Ignition Selection

Attributes: Caused by lightning
Location: South Fork Merced watershed, Yosemite NP
Time period: 1994-2004

TIP

If the fire occurrence (ignition point) data don't contain all the attribute information necessary to select potential simulation ignitions, it may be possible to supplement it with attribute information contained in a digital fire atlas (polygon) dataset.

Identifying ignitions that may have exhibited significant spread had they not been suppressed can be complicated. Many of the ignitions found in the fire occurrence files wouldn't have become established wildfires due to fuel discontinuity, high fuel moistures, subsequent weather conditions (e.g., significant rain), or other spread inhibiting environmental conditions. Therefore, it is generally necessary to refine the set of potential simulation ignitions with additional selection criteria. Many criteria can be used, singly or in conjunction with one another, to make these decisions. These include basic weather conditions, fuel moistures, fire weather indices (e.g., ERC or SC), final fire size, underlying fuel models, surrounding fuel continuity, elevation, and expert opinion. In the case study, ERC was used to help identify which ignitions to model but SC or Burning Index (BI) could have been used instead. The best approach is to determine the weather conditions, fire weather indices, underlying fuel model, final fire size, and so on, for each ignition and consult with local fire management experts to define the criteria under which an ignition is most likely to spread.

EXAMPLE

Ignition Selection Criteria

In the case study, a combination of ERC, the underlying fuel model, expert opinion, and attribute information, such as final fire size, were used to make the ignition selection. Specifically, fuel models were divided in terms of rate of spread into "fast" and "slow" categories. For example, a fully cured tall grass fuel model was considered "fast," whereas a very low load conifer litter fuel model was considered "slow." Some fuel types were considered slow early in the fire season and fast later in the fire season once their fuels had cured. The use of these criteria identified 10 ignitions out of 34 candidates (Fig. 6).

Criteria for inclusion as an ignition likely to spread:

1) Occurred in a "fast" fuel model and ERC > 15th percentile
2) Occurred in a "slow" fuel model and ERC > 50th percentile
3) ERC exceeds the threshold value of 90th percentile at some point between the ignition date and the end of the fire season
4) Exceptions: The above are general criteria. Any ignition that had other attributes (e.g., final fire size) indicating the potential for significant spread was considered a candidate as well.

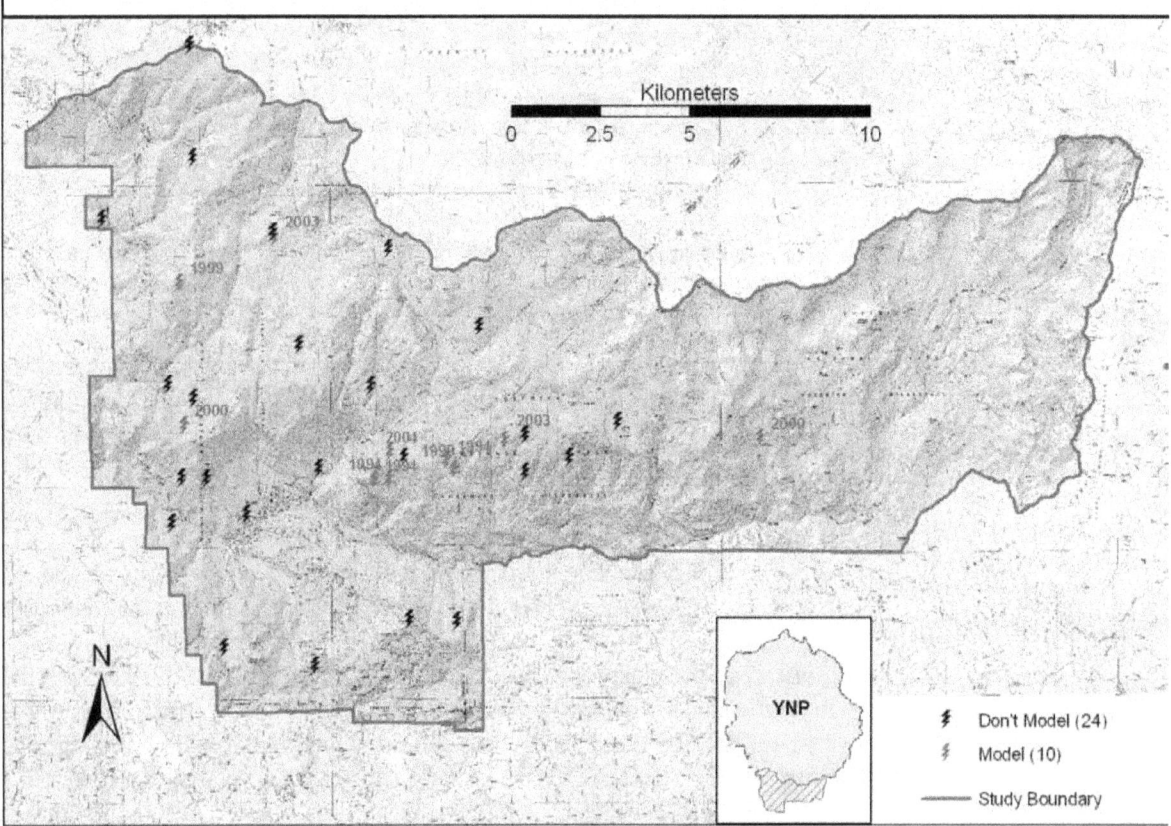

Figure 6. Potential simulation ignitions, South Fork Merced watershed.

Once the ignitions with potential for spread have been selected, their coordinates need to be manipulated into a file format that is compatible with the fire growth model. It is necessary to create a separate coordinate file for each individual ignition. FARSITE accepts multiple types of ignition files including ASCII text and shapefiles. ASCII files are recommended due to their small size and simplicity. See the FARSITE help file for formatting information.

Fuels Data

Fuels data represent the medium through which the modeled fires will spread. They have a significant impact on fire behavior and effects. Therefore, care should be given to their acquisition and development. See Stratton (2009) for a thorough discussion of considerations.

Acquiring fuels data: The FARSITE and FlamMap models require the construction of a LCP (landscape) file. Required fuels inputs for a LCP file include surface fuel models and canopy cover. Modeling crown fire requires the following additional inputs: canopy height, canopy base height, and canopy bulk density. Modeling emissions with FARSITE requires duff and coarse woody debris layers be included as well. Fuels data are best obtained from the agency responsible for the study site. If they are unavailable from the responsible agency, they may be available from the LANDFIRE project (Rollins 2009; http://www.landfire.gov/dataproduct_overview.php). Precompiled LCP files can be downloaded from LANDFIRE, complete with topography and surface and canopy fuels. If fuels data are unavailable or not of sufficient quality, it may be necessary to develop the data by crosswalking any available vegetation data. For the case study, the latest vegetation data were obtained from the land management agency and, in cooperation with managers and scientists, a crosswalk was developed from vegetation type to a set of surface fuel models (Scott and Burgan 2005; Fig. 7).

Preparing fuels data: Some of the most important inputs for fire growth modeling describe surface and canopy fuels. It is important to determine when the fuels data were developed and if they have been updated or manipulated. These data are generally derived from the underlying vegetation data, which usually are at least partly based on remotely sensed data such as satellite or aerial imagery. It is desirable to use fuels data (and any other time sensitive data) that most accurately reflect the starting year of the simulation. If the year of the imagery capture differs from the desired starting year, modifying the input data to reflect an earlier or later date (e.g., updating fuels to reflect disturbances or successional changes that occurred between the chosen start date and the imagery capture date) will improve the accuracy of the data. Similar modifications may need to be made to canopy cover and the other crown fuels data.

EXAMPLE

Surface Fuel Development and Manipulation

The imagery used to develop vegetation data for Yosemite National Park was captured in 1997. The proposed start date for the case study retrospective fire simulation was 1994. To better reflect fuel conditions in 1994 any fires that occurred between 1994 and 1996 were "unburned." This was accomplished by replacing the vegetation classification for those areas that burned between 1994 and 1996 with data from the park's previous vegetation coverage. The resulting vegetation data were then crosswalked to surface fuels (Fig. 7).

Initial (1994) Surface Fuel Models

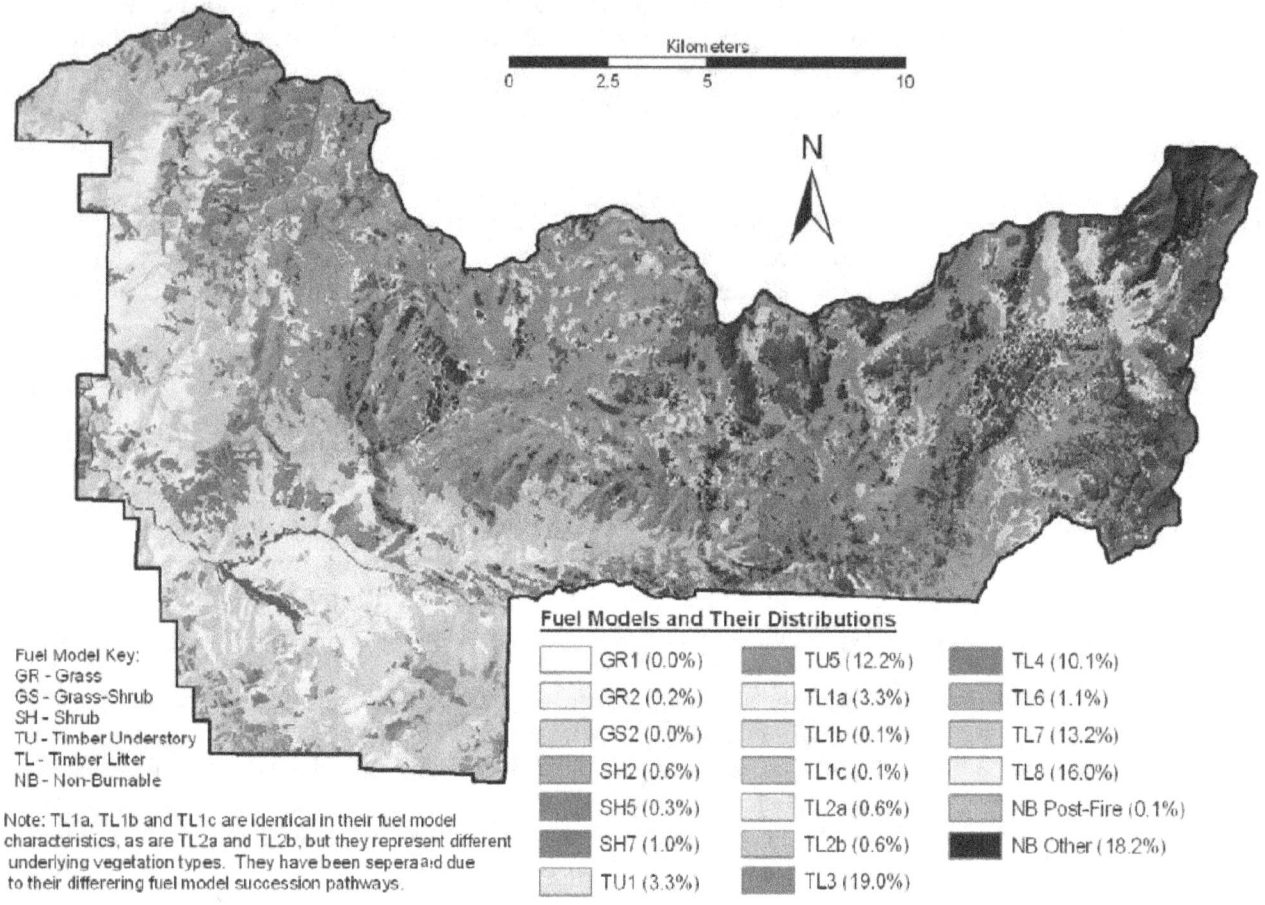

Fuel Model Key:
GR - Grass
GS - Grass-Shrub
SH - Shrub
TU - Timber Understory
TL - Timber Litter
NB - Non-Burnable

Note: TL1a, TL1b and TL1c are identical in their fuel model characteristics, as are TL2a and TL2b, but they represent different underlying vegetation types. They have been seperaad due to their differering fuel model succession pathways.

Fuel Models and Their Distributions

GR1 (0.0%)	TU5 (12.2%)	TL4 (10.1%)
GR2 (0.2%)	TL1a (3.3%)	TL6 (1.1%)
GS2 (0.0%)	TL1b (0.1%)	TL7 (13.2%)
SH2 (0.6%)	TL1c (0.1%)	TL8 (16.0%)
SH5 (0.3%)	TL2a (0.6%)	NB Post-Fire (0.1%)
SH7 (1.0%)	TL2b (0.6%)	NB Other (18.2%)
TU1 (3.3%)	TL3 (19.0%)	

Figure 7. Surface fuel models, South Fork Merced watershed.

Topographic Data

Elevation, slope, and aspect data are required elements of a LCP file and can be obtained from various sources, including the responsible agency and the National Elevation Dataset (http://seamless.usgs.gov/index.php). The elevation dataset can be used to create the slope and aspect data using a GIS program such as ArcGIS (ESRI 2005).

To build a LCP file, all spatial inputs (fuels, elevation, etc.) must be converted to ASCII format. Conversion methodology will vary depending on the format of the original data. For example, if the fuels data reside in an ArcInfo grid, the "gridascii" command in GRID can be used to convert the grid into an ASCII file, as can the "raster to ASCII" tool in ArcGIS. The original files must have a common projection, format, cell size, and origin (the same minimum X and Y coordinates) before conversion to ASCII files.

Fire Atlas Data

Historical fire atlas data are used for many purposes in retrospective fire modeling including updating fuels data, modifying fire spread, and as input to metrics used to measure the impact of alternative management strategies.

Fire Atlas 1930 - 2004

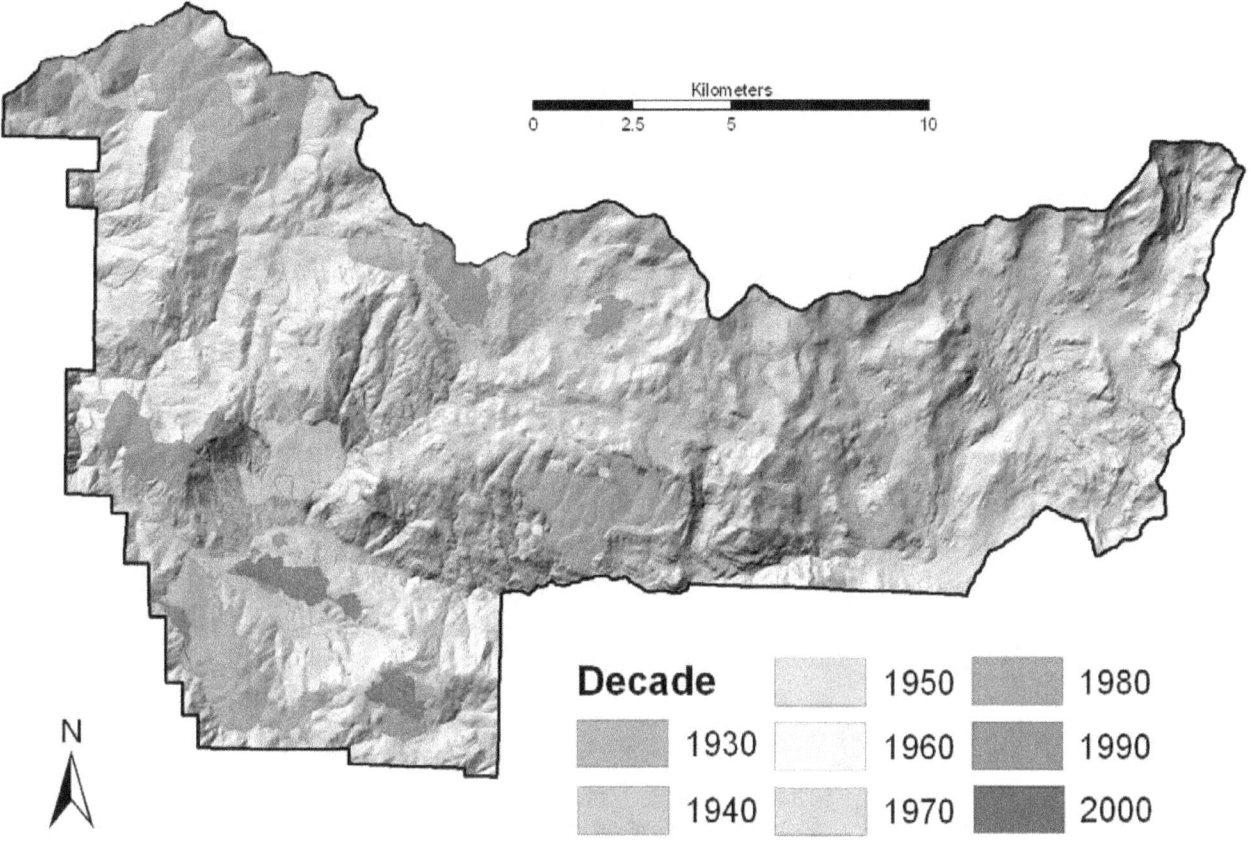

Figure 8. 1930-2004 fire atlas for the South Fork Merced watershed.

Acquiring fire atlas data: Fire atlas data (aka fire history data) are generally polygon spatial data representing the final perimeters and other attributes (e.g., dates) of historical fires. They are usually available from the management agency responsible for the study area. When calculating a fire regime departure measure such as FRID, it is important to obtain as much historical fire data as possible, as these data are integral to calculating these measures. For example, in the case study analysis in the South Fork Merced watershed, approximately 550 fire perimeters from 1930 through 2004 were obtained (Fig. 8). Because the majority of these fires were less than one acre, they will not be readily apparent in figure 8. This is a very extensive dataset with a long period of record. Such extensive data may not be available for all areas. It is important to state that any fire atlas used for the purpose of retrospective fire modeling should include prescribed fires as well as wildland fires. This is important because, from the landscape's perspective, there is little difference whether the fires were planned or not.

Preparing fire atlas data: Fire atlas data are used in retrospective fire modeling for three purposes: to update fuels layers between simulation years, create barriers to fire spread within FARSITE, and calculate the fire regime departures (FRID, FRCC) that enable comparisons between alternative landscapes. Multiple sub-atlases must be derived from the complete fire atlas for these purposes; these sub-atlases are listed below.

1. Historical fire atlas: This is an atlas containing the perimeters of the earliest fires available through the last year of the retrospective simulation. The historical fire atlas contains fires that contributed to the realized landscape.

2. Truncated historical fire atlas: This is an atlas that contains fires from the earliest year available up to the first year of the simulation. Modeled fire perimeters and the appropriate real fire perimeters will be added to this atlas after all simulations are complete to create a hypothetical fire atlas. This sub-atlas will contain fires that contributed to the hypothetical landscape.

3. Individual real fires: Each real fire that occurred during the simulation period must be extracted into its own, separate file. These files will be used to modify the landscape during fire growth modeling (i.e., to create barriers to fire spread), update fuels after each simulation year and rebuild an atlas containing both simulated and real fires.

TIP

Fire Atlas Manipulation

Some fire atlases include very small fires. To expedite the retrospective modeling process, we recommend setting a minimum threshold, between 1 and 10 acres, and eliminating fires smaller than this threshold. Eliminating these small fires will reduce the time it takes to prepare the data and perform the analysis without having a large impact on the results. When using FARSITE as the fire growth model, a "shapefile" is the recommended format for the fire atlases.

Example

Fire Atlas Preparation

Historical fire atlas: contains all real fires (1930-2004, 555 perimeters)
Truncated historical fire atlas: contains real fires only up until simulation start year (1930-1993, 439 perimeters)
Individual real fires: one shapefile per fire 1994-2004 (min. 1 acre)

Optional Data

Wildland fire severity data: Wherever available, severity data for real fires should be used to help update fuels between simulation years. The local management agency is the best starting point for finding these data. Another good option is the Monitoring Trends in Burn Severity project (http://mtbs.gov), which has burn severity data for most large fires (>1000 acres) and some smaller fires dating back to 1984. For those wildland fires for which there are no data, assumptions about the severity must be made. In the case study, a moderate severity was assumed for existing atlas fires when severity data were unavailable.

Fire Return Intervals (FRI): The calculation of Fire Return Interval Departure (FRID) requires FRI and fire atlas data (discussed above). FRI data may be obtained from the management agency, or it may be necessary to extract it from the scientific literature. Contacting a fire ecologist familiar with the study area may be the best way to discover what data are available. FRI data may be formatted as a table of return intervals by vegetation type or as spatial data. Tabular FRI data can generally be used to create spatial FRI data by crosswalking vegetation GIS data (Fig. 9). This spatial (raster) FRI data will be important to the calculation of FRID when comparing alternative landscapes.

Median Fire Return Interval

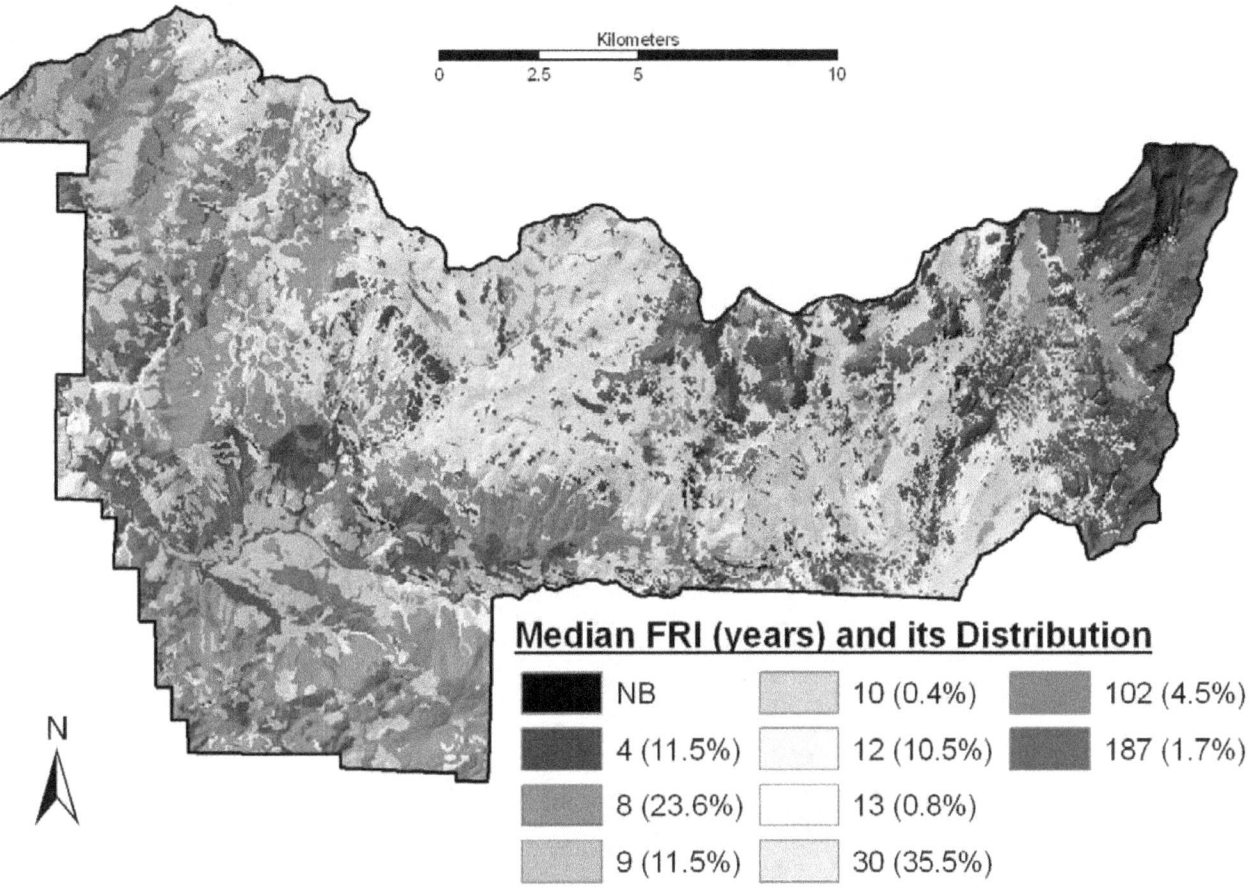

Figure 9. Fire Return Intervals for South Fork Merced watershed.

Other data: Other data may be required depending on the models, outputs, and methodologies selected. For example, duff and coarse woody debris data are required to model emissions with FARSITE, and the optional crown fire inputs are required to model crown fire.

Modeling and Analysis

The retrospective fire modeling process has a few generic steps: defining parameters and preparing input data (as described above), modeling fire spread and behavior, updating fuels layers based on modeled and real fire and fuel accumulation, repeating the process, and comparing the resultant alternative landscapes. In order to generate a clear picture of the sequential steps it is helpful to draw up a timeline of events.

Defining Timeline

For each year of the simulation, a timeline of all events during the fire season that can affect the simulation of fire growth must be created. These events include ignition dates, weather events, occurrence of real fires and the crossing of thresholds defining when fire growth should be simulated, paused, or stopped. The timeline can be developed using the daily listing of fire weather index values, rain amounts, dates of ignitions, and any other information that may affect fire growth simulation. This timeline can be referred to during the fire growth modeling process. Note that the thresholds used in the case study were based on local manager opinion and should not be applied uncritically to a different study area.

EXAMPLE

Simulation Timeline

Date	Event	Action
June 27	Calder ignition	Import ignition
July 2	Grove wildfire	Import perimeter as barrier
July 25	ERC above 90th %	Start simulation
August 1	Bug ignition	Pause, import ignition, restart
August 4	ERC above 98th %	Pause, change burning period*, restart
August 8	ERC below 98th %	Pause, change burning period*, restart
August 12	ERC below 90th %	Pause
August 25	Jones ignition	Import ignition
September 3	ERC above 90th %	Restart
September 6	Axe wildfire	Pause, import as barrier, restart
September 9	ERC below 90th %	Pause
October 3	ERC above 90th %	Restart
October 15	Fire-ending rain event	End simulation

*In the case study the length of the daily burning period changed when ERC exceeded the 98th percentile (see FARSITE help file for definition of burning period).

In the above example, fire growth is simulated only on those days when the ERC is above the 90th percentile. This translates into 36 simulation days divided into three simulation "periods" (July 25-August 12, September 3-September 9 and October 3-October 15). The criteria that determine when fire growth is simulated are defined by the user (as described in the weather data section), as is the definition of a fire-ending precipitation event. Because modeled fires and fuel succession can impact events in a particular simulation year's timeline, it shouldn't be developed until after the previous year has been modeled and fuel succession is applied.

Revisiting Ignition Selection

The timeline created in the previous step can inform which ignitions need to be simulated for the retrospective fire analysis. In addition to the selection criteria described in the "Preparing ignition data" section above, ignitions can be eliminated during the modeling process for other reasons. They can be eliminated if a modeled fire from earlier in the same simulation year burns over their location before they occurred, or if a previous year's modeled fire burns over their location and the fuels haven't recovered yet. Similarly, real fires can be eliminated in the same fashion. In other words, some of the ignitions originally selected for modeling and the ignition points for "real" fires may fall on areas that became unburnable due to a previously modeled fire. These ignitions can be left out of the analysis. It is for this reason that each year's timeline should be prepared only after the previous year's simulation and post-season fuel succession modeling is complete. The ignitions and real fires that can be eliminated from the analysis can be determined by identifying the fuel conditions at the time and place of their occurrence.

Modeling Fire Growth and Behavior

Once the ignitions have been refined to include only those that likely would have become established wildfires, they are used in the fire growth model as starting points for predicting fire spread and the final fire perimeter. The following instructions and descriptions are based on the use of FARSITE as the fire growth model. When using a program other than FARSITE to model fire growth, the following procedures can be used as a conceptual guide.

Modeling fire growth using FARSITE is deceptively simple to implement. With the assistance of the FARSITE tutorial and help file, anyone can run the model, but it takes training and experience to understand the underlying assumptions and limitations and to use it most effectively. Before this tool is used for retrospective fire modeling, we highly recommend appropriate training (e.g., taking the S-495 "Geospatial Fire Analysis, Interpretation and Application" course) and experience, or at least access to someone who has these. While information specific to using FARSITE for retrospective modeling is covered in this guide, instruction on the correct general operation of FARSITE is beyond the scope of this document and will not be presented. Details on setting up a FARSITE run can be found in the FARSITE tutorial and help files. General guidelines on LCP (landscape file) critiques, FARSITE parameters, and FARSITE calibration can be found in Stratton (2009). The following instructions assume a basic familiarity with FARSITE and fire growth modeling.

A note on calibrating FARSITE: Calibrating FARSITE to known fire spread and behavior will greatly increase confidence in its outputs. Calibration for historical ignitions is a more complicated task than calibrating for an actual and ongoing fire event because most historical ignitions were successfully suppressed by initial attack before growing to any substantial size and thereby providing information on natural fire spread. Historical fires that weren't suppressed or for which the suppression tactics are well known are particularly valuable for calibrating FARSITE parameters. When progression data are available for historical fires, be sure to consider that they may not necessarily be representative of the ignition(s) you are modeling due to differences in location, fuels, and weather conditions. Broad guidelines for model calibration can be found in Stratton (2006, 2009). If sufficient fire spread data aren't available, consult with someone who has experience modeling fire in or near the study area for guidance on the adjustments for localized calibration. Especially useful are "starting point" rate of spread adjustments and burn periods (see "Calculating fire weather index percentiles" under the "Preparing weather data" section above for an explanation of burn periods) under varying fire weather conditions. These are generally based on the local fire modeler's experience. If threshold conditions (e.g., a minimum ERC) are being used to determine when to simulate fire growth, calibrations should be made with these conditions in mind.

TIP

Using Custom Fuel Models Instead of FARSITE Adjustment Files

The use of the adjustment (.adj) file is the quickest and crudest way of calibrating FARSITE, but the adjustment file only affects rate of spread and not other fire behavior characteristics. If other fire behavior characteristics, such as flame length, are of concern, custom fuel models and/or conversion files can be used to adjust modeled fire behavior (for example, use the "tuning" feature of FARSITE's custom fuel model editor). When a fuel model is "tuned" to change rate of spread, the adjustment is reflected in other fire behavior characteristics as well. The resultant custom fuel model file (.fmd) can be used in conjunction with a fuel model conversion file (.cnv) to adjust fire behavior without the need to incorporate the custom fuel model into the fuels data layer. See FARSITE's help file for more information on creating custom fuel model, conversion and adjustment files.

Build and Load the LCP File

LCP files can be created using FARSITE's landscape utility (Input > Landscape Utilities > Generate Landscape File). Creation of fuels and topography inputs is described above. Select the correct units for each input and set the latitude for the study area.

Project Inputs

Load the project inputs (Input > Project Inputs) (Fig. 10). The LCP, adjustment, fuel moisture, weather, wind and burn period files are minimally necessary inputs (the burn period file is not required but is almost certainly appropriate; see the FARSITE help file for explanations of why burn period files are important).

Project Parameters

Parameters should be defined based on general FARSITE knowledge, calibration results, local fire growth simulation knowledge, and output desires. Set the project parameters for the simulation (Model > Parameters, Model > Fire Behavior Options, Simulate > Options, and Simulate > Duration) (Fig. 11). Select whether or not crown fire and spotting will be simulated (Model > Fire Behavior Options). In the case study, crown fire was simulated, but spotting was not (Fig. 12). Simulation duration should be set from the beginning of the burn period on the first day of fire growth to the beginning of the burn period on the day *after* the final day of fire growth. Refer to the timeline and burn period times to define the simulation duration. If emissions are being modeled using FARSITE, set the post-frontal combustion parameters (Model > Post-Frontal Combustion). Other model parameters (e.g., fire acceleration, dead fuel moisture) can be set at the user's discretion.

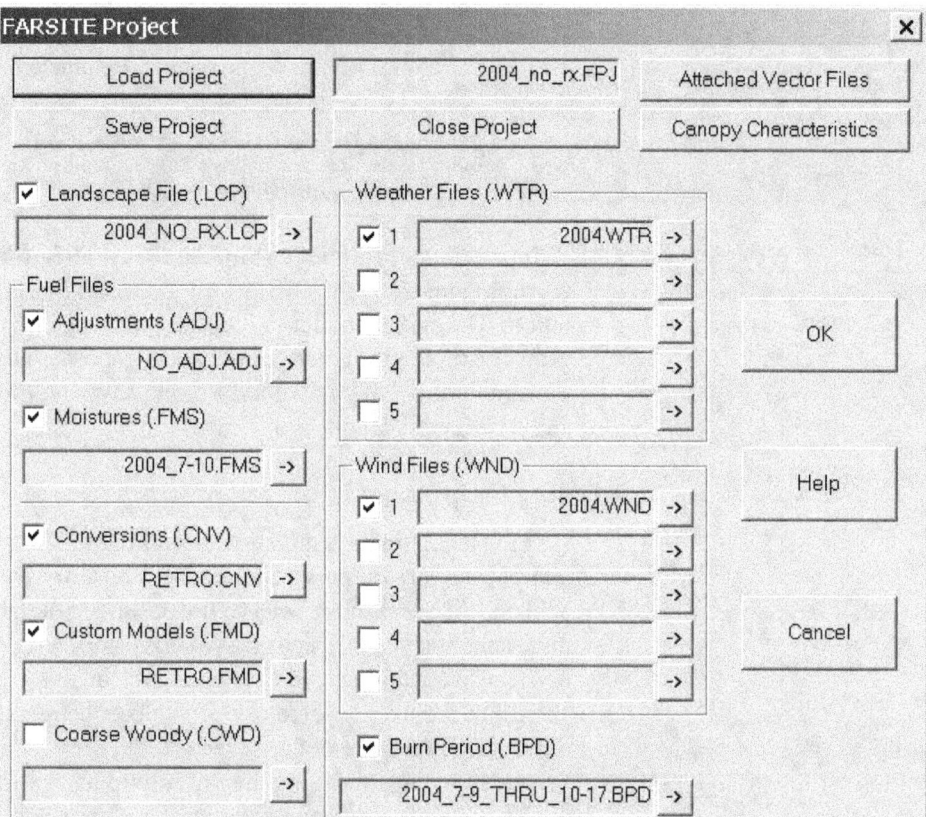

Figure 10. FARSITE project inputs.

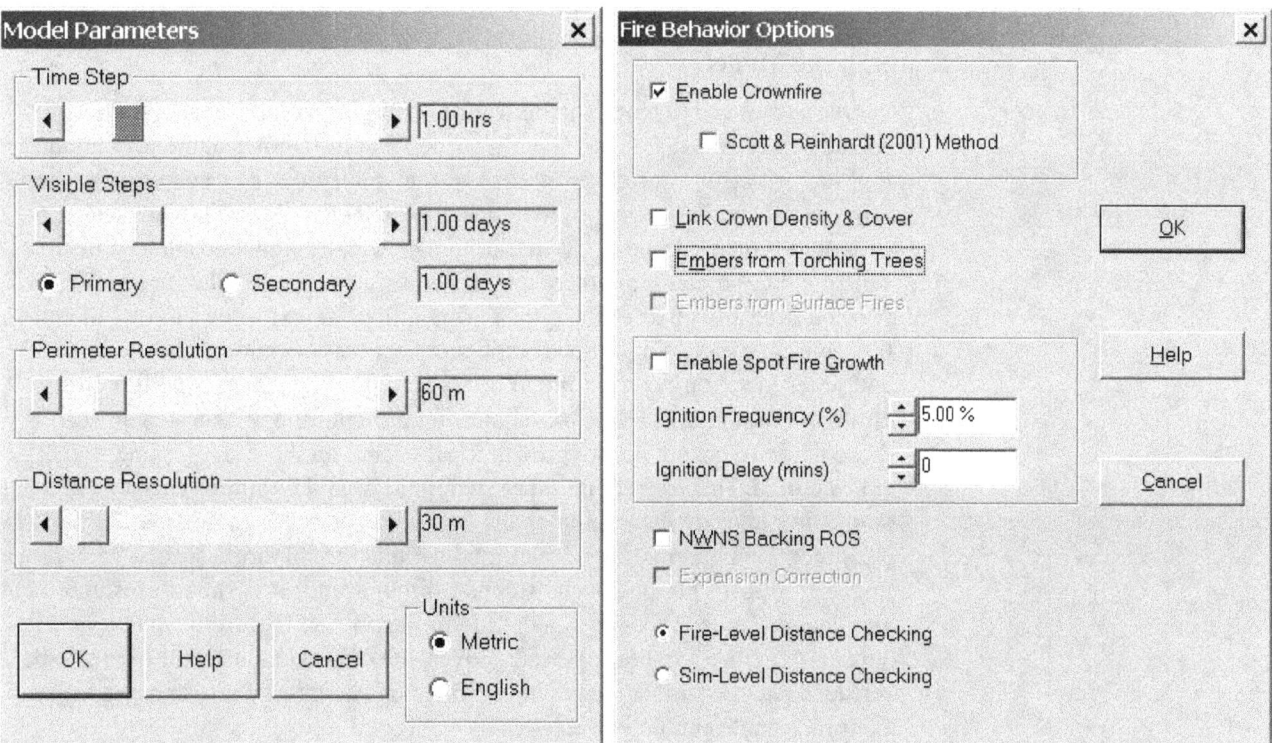

Figure 11. FARSITE model parameters.

Figure 12. FARSITE fire behavior options.

TIP

FARSITE Parameters

For longer simulations, it may be necessary to use coarser model parameters to ensure reasonable simulation times. This is a tradeoff with output precision. A one day visible time step is probably the most useful for long duration retrospective simulations.

Import *initial* ignitions (Simulate > Modify Map > Import Ignitions) and barriers (Simulate > Modify Map > Import Barriers) after "initiating" the simulation. The initial ignitions are those that occur prior to the first day of fire growth simulation. Later ignitions are imported at the appropriate time during the simulation. Now is a good time to save the project (Input > Save Project) and a bookmark (Input > Bookmarks).

Selecting Outputs

Prior to starting a simulation, select outputs (Output > Export and Outputs) and choose any outputs of interest or those necessary for future modeling or analysis. At a minimum, select a fire perimeter output. For the fire perimeter outputs, enabling "visible steps only," "save perimeters as polygons," and "exclude barriers" is recommended to facilitate the analysis of results. Raster outputs are chosen at the user's discretion. If a subsequent analysis of fuel succession requires some measure of fire severity (e.g., crown fire occurrence, flame length), be sure to include it among the raster outputs.

Smoke emission estimates can be obtained by enabling an output table (Output > Data Tables > Post-frontal Combustion). The table for each emission of interest (e.g., PM 2.5) can be saved as a text file for later manipulation and analysis after the FARSITE run is complete. Change emission type and save emission files by right-clicking within the table.

Running the Model

Due to the need to modify parameters and import ignitions and barriers to fire spread (e.g., areas that have recently burned and have not accumulated enough fuel to burn again) during the course of the simulation, it is necessary to step through the simulation day-by-day using FARSITE's "Step Through" function (Simulate > Step Through). "Step Through" runs the simulation one visible time step at a time. In addition, there may be times when the simulation needs to be put "on-hold." To pause fire growth simulation for extended periods of time (i.e., multiple days) in FARSITE the simplest way should be to set start and end times in the burn period file to 00:00 on days when there is no fire growth. Unfortunately, FARSITE still simulates fire growth for one time step on each of those days. To ensure no fire growth at all occurs on those days, some trickery is is required. This trickery involves stepping FARSITE through each day of the simulation until the beginning of the "on-hold" period. A new adjustment file (.adj) containing zeros for all fuel models must be imported so that each day of the "on-hold" period can be stepped through until it is time to resume the simulation. Zeros in the adjustment file prevent FARSITE from simulating fire spread. After the "on-hold" period is over, the original adjustment file must be reloaded and the simulation resumed. There can be many pause and resume actions in a single simulation year.

While other pauses of fire growth may be required (e.g., to modify parameters, import ignitions, or barriers to fire spread), such pauses can be handled with the step-through method (without importing the "zero .adj file")

TIP

Minimizing Active Simulation Periods

If you are using fire weather thresholds to define when a fire will or will not grow, you can minimize the number of active simulation periods by defining the threshold as "crossed" only when the condition persists for multiple days. For example, in the case study, a pause was not implemented unless ERC dropped and remained below the 90th percentile threshold for two consecutive days and a resumption of fire growth was not enacted unless ERC remained above the 90th percentile for the same period of time.

Run the FARSITE simulation using the step-through option making the appropriate imports and parameter adjustments as necessary until the end date is reached (Fig. 13). If smoke emissions were modeled, save the files (right-click within the emissions table) for the emissions components of interest (e.g., PM 2.5, PM 10, or CO^2). These files can then be manipulated and analyzed using a spreadsheet (e.g., Excel) or other program. With the appropriate manipulation, they can be attached to FARSITE's fire growth vector file as attributes. After the smoke emissions output tables are saved, "terminate" the simulation and review all FARSITE outputs to make sure the results seem reasonable (Fig. 14). Manipulate the FARSITE outputs into the forms and formats necessary to implement the selected method of fuel succession.

Updating Model Inputs

Surface Fuels

As described above, fuel succession can be simulated in a number of different ways. This section describes the methods used in the case study, but the general ideas are applicable with other methods as well. Drivers of the fuel succession model used in the case study include pre-fire fuel model, fire severity data (modeled and real), time since last fire, state transitions for each fuel type for each fire severity class, fuel accumulation rates, and post-disturbance recovery rates (Fig. 1).

For the modeled fires in the case study, the approximation of severity was driven by two factors. The first was the FARSITE output "Crown Fire Activity," a categorical output divided up into surface fire, passive crown fire (torching) and active crown fire. These data were used as a proxy for fire severity where surface = low severity, passive = moderate severity, and active = high severity. Crown fire activity was chosen as the proxy because it has the capacity to approximate what would be seen from an overhead, remotely sensed perspective. The use of remote sensing (e.g., satellite imagery) is the most common way that real-world severity data are obtained. It is generally dependent on comparing before and after images and determining the amount of change between the two (Key & Benson 2006, Thode 2005). The second, and probably more important factor, is that the fuel succession model only allows for certain severities in each fuel type. This was based on the assumption that certain fuel types would only burn with particular severities. This addresses a number of problems, including severities in fuel types without canopy (e.g. grasses and shrubs), where using

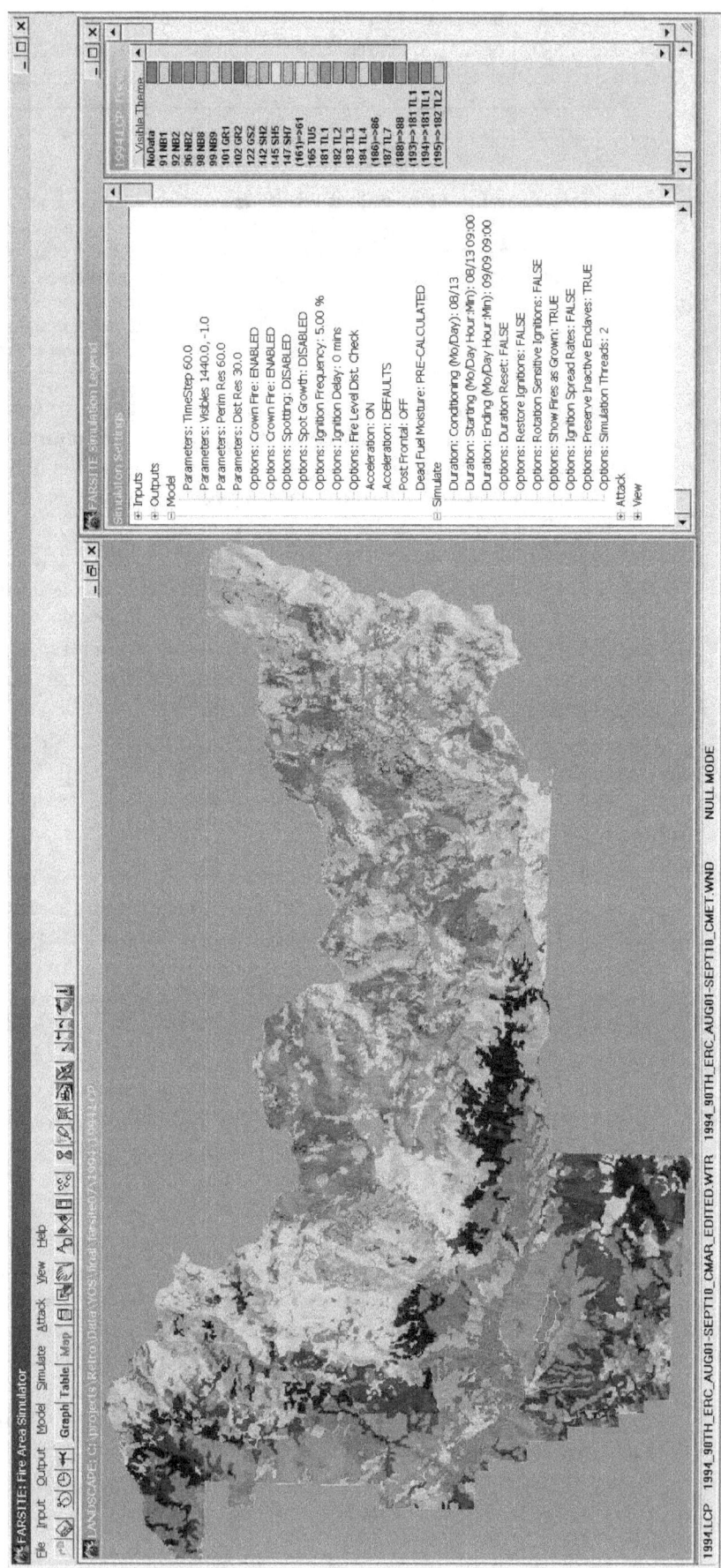

Figure 13. FARSITE.

1994 Modeled Fire Perimeters

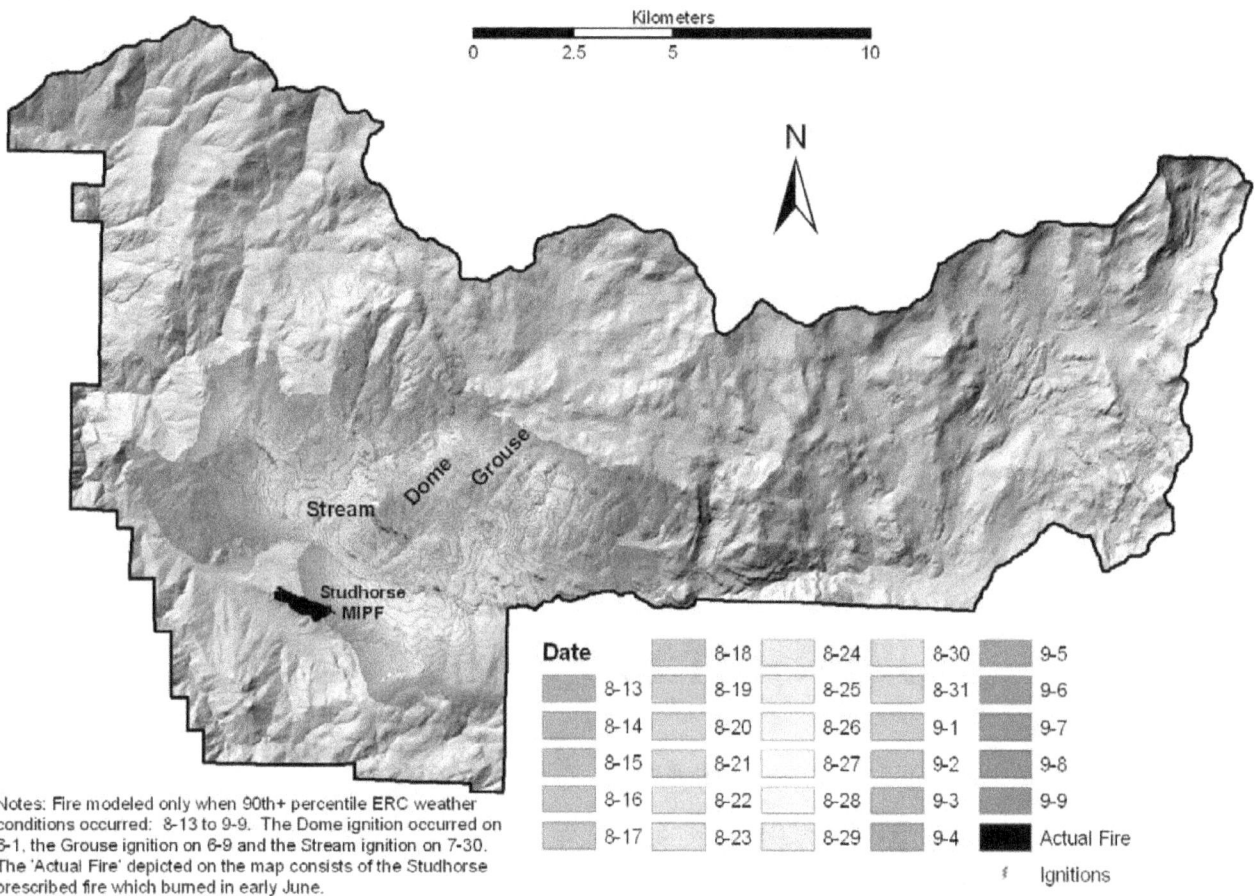

Figure 14. Simulated fire growth.

Notes: Fire modeled only when 90th+ percentile ERC weather conditions occurred: 8-13 to 9-9. The Dome ignition occurred on 6-1, the Grouse ignition on 6-9 and the Stream ignition on 7-30. The 'Actual Fire' depicted on the map consists of the Studhorse prescribed fire which burned in early June.

crown fire activity as a proxy for fire severity would always result in low severities (surface fire).

Some examples include the Grass 2 (GR2; Low load, dry climate grass) fuel model that, from a remote sensing perspective, would appear to have burned with high severity due to large differences in the pre- and post-fire images. Without analyst intervention, these areas may be classified as such. Using crown fire activity as a proxy will result in the area always being classified as a low severity (surface) fire which is considered to be a more accurate classification. Another example would be Timber Litter 1 (TL1; Low load, compact conifer litter), which is restricted to burning in low or moderate severity fires, because the amount of surface fuels and the structure of the canopy of the underlying vegetation types are not considered sufficient to support a high severity (active crown) fire.

The fuel succession model is run using both the modeled fires and the real fires that occurred during the simulation year as inputs. Real fires include any fire that actually occurred whether it was a wildfire or a prescribed fire. The locations of modeled fires should be compared to the locations of any real fires that occurred that year. If there is overlap, it should be determined whether the modeled fire arrived at the real fire's ignition location before or after that ignition occurred. If it arrived before, the real fire can be removed from the fuel update process and the results analyses because it would have been eliminated due to fuel consumption at its point of ignition. When evaluating the inclusion of prescribed fires in the fuel succession process, the ignition locations viability shouldn't be the deciding factor. Instead, the amount of the prescribed fire's area burned by a prior modeled fire should be taken into account. Usually it will come down to the user's judgment whether or not to include the prescribed fire in the succession process.

EXAMPLE

Fuel Succession

The surface fuel succession model used in the case study is implemented using an Arc Macro Language (AML) script within ArcGIS Workstation. Inputs include the pre-fire fuel model, fire severity data (modeled and real), and crosswalk parameters including time since last fire, succession steps for the four potential fire conditions (no fire, low, moderate and high severities), rates of fuel accumulation, and post-fire fuel recovery.

The outputs include next year's surface fuel model (Fig. 15) and all the inputs necessary to simulate the subsequent year's succession with the exception of the fire severity grid.

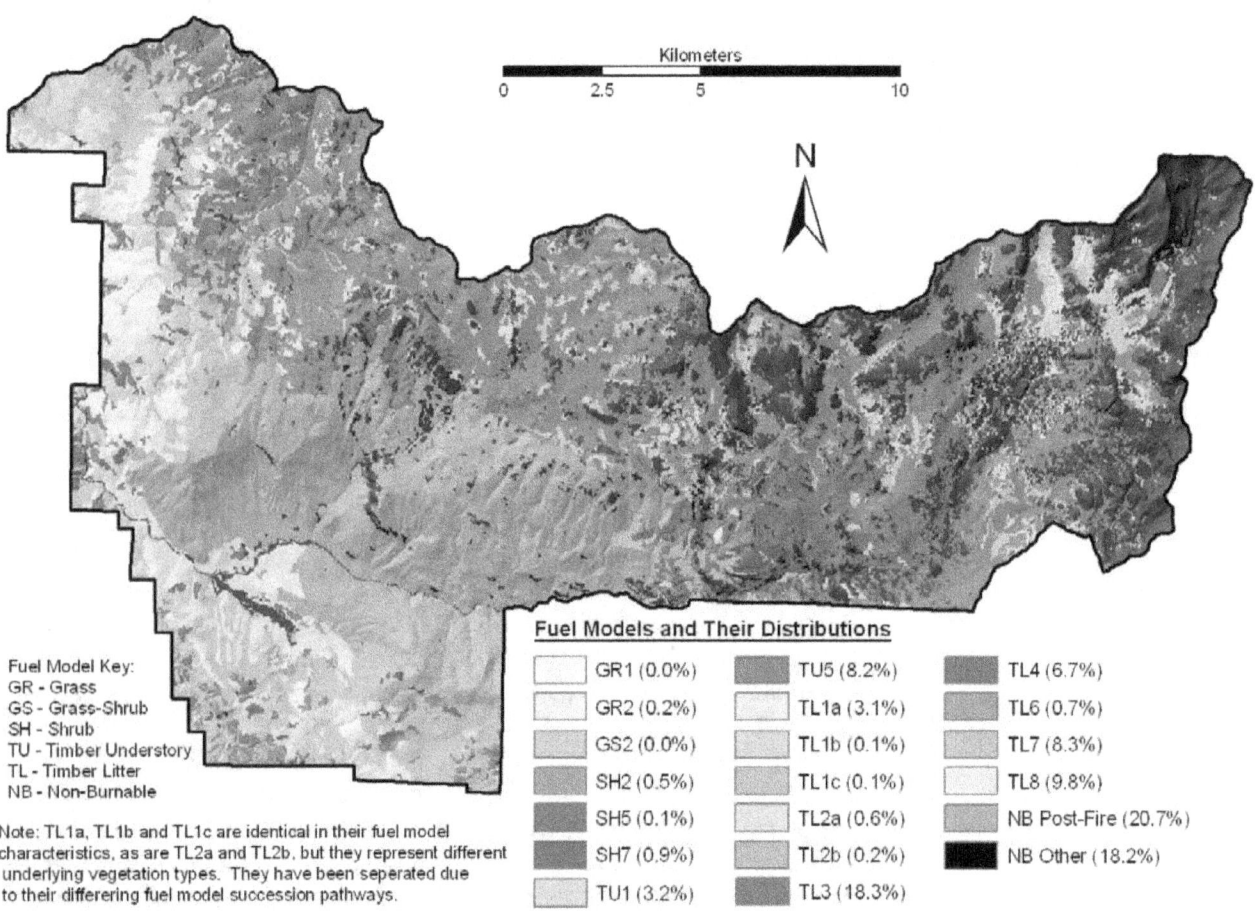

1995 Surface Fuel Models

Fuel Model Key:
GR - Grass
GS - Grass-Shrub
SH - Shrub
TU - Timber Understory
TL - Timber Litter
NB - Non-Burnable

Note: TL1a, TL1b and TL1c are identical in their fuel model characteristics, as are TL2a and TL2b, but they represent different underlying vegetation types. They have been seperated due to their differering fuel model succession pathways.

Fuel Models and Their Distributions

GR1 (0.0%)	TU5 (8.2%)	TL4 (6.7%)
GR2 (0.2%)	TL1a (3.1%)	TL6 (0.7%)
GS2 (0.0%)	TL1b (0.1%)	TL7 (8.3%)
SH2 (0.5%)	TL1c (0.1%)	TL8 (9.8%)
SH5 (0.1%)	TL2a (0.6%)	NB Post-Fire (20.7%)
SH7 (0.9%)	TL2b (0.2%)	NB Other (18.2%)
TU1 (3.2%)	TL3 (18.3%)	

Figure 15. Surface fuels after the modeled 1994 fire season.

USDA Forest Service RMRS-GTR-236WWW. 2010.

Canopy Fuels

Canopy fuel updates should be performed where and when the canopy may have changed due to modeled or real fire. The user must decide when and how to update the canopy fuels. Changes can be made using a simple rule set in a GIS. For example, a crosswalk can be developed using FARSITE's crown fire activity output and assumptions about how crown fire activity affects canopy attributes.

EXAMPLE

Canopy Fuel Crosswalk

<u>No fire:</u> No change
<u>Surface fire:</u> No change
<u>Passive crown fire:</u> 25% reduction in canopy cover and 25% reduction in crown bulk density.
<u>Active crown fire:</u> 95% reduction in canopy cover and 100% reduction in crown bulk density

---

Alternatively, canopy fuel updates can be modeled using various fuel consumption and fuel accumulation models such as FOFEM and FVS-FFE.

Duff and Coarse Woody Debris

Updating duff and coarse woody debris can be done in much the same manner as updating canopy fuels. Simplistic user defined crosswalks or more involved fuel consumption and accumulation models can be used.

Update Fire Growth and Behavior Model Inputs

All FARSITE inputs affected by fuel succession need to be updated in the LCP file before simulating the subsequent year of fires in the retrospective analysis. New raster fuels data need to be exported into an ASCII format; this should be completed after modeling is complete for each year in the simulation.

TIP

Updating the FARSITE Project

The easiest way to create a new FARSITE LCP file is to update the previous one and save it with a new name. However, using the same approach with the FARSITE project file is not recommended due to the risk of forgetting to change a parameter from the previous year's value and invalidating the results. Instead, the user should update the previous year's LCP file with the new fuels and save it with a new file name. Then start a new FARSITE project, load the new LCP file, and populate all parameters, options, and other inputs as outlined in the "Fire growth" section above.

Before importing the next modeling year's initial ignitions and barriers to fire spread, overlay them on the latest fuel model using a GIS. Some of the selected ignitions and the ignition points for other "real" fires may now fall on areas that are currently unburnable due to a previous year's modeled fire. Those that do can be left out of the analysis.

Repeating Modeling Cycle

Once the new project (for the new modeling year) is parameterized and saved, run FARSITE in the same manner as the previous year. Continue this cycle of fire growth simulation and fuel succession through the final fire year in the retrospective simulation period. Update the last LCP file with the results of the final fuel succession modeling before comparing the alternative landscapes.

Comparing Alternative Landscapes

Fire suppression impacts can be measured by comparing the hypothetical landscape (in the case study this is the landscape that would have resulted had the suppressed ignitions been allowed to burn) to the realized landscape (the landscape that resulted as a consequence of fire suppression). The impacts quantified for the case study include FRID and flame length.

Fire Regime Departure

Fire Return Interval Departure (FRID): FRID data are developed by determining how many years have passed since an area last burned and dividing that number by the characteristic Fire Return Interval (FRI) of the underlying vegetation. Time since last burn is calculated using a fire atlas. To compare the alternative landscapes there are two atlases necessary: the hypothetical atlas and the realized atlas.

Building the hypothetical fire atlas: The first step in calculating FRID is to build a new fire atlas to represent the alternative fire management strategy. This fire atlas should incorporate the modeled fire perimeters and those of real fires that weren't eliminated by the modeled fires. This is accomplished by using a GIS to merge these modeled and real fire perimeters with the "truncated historical fire atlas" (which contains fires from the earliest year available through the year prior to the first simulation; see the "Preparing fire atlas data" section above). Once the additional fire perimeters are appended, it is important to populate at least the year attribute of the resulting fire atlas to facilitate the FRID calculation.

Calculating a hypothetical FRID: The "hypothetical fire atlas" and the "realized fire atlas" can then be used to create a "last burned" raster layer for each alternative landscape. Creating a last burned dataset can be accomplished in a number of ways using a GIS and should be performed by someone with GIS analysis experience. Most methods will involve ensuring that the fire perimeters are layered in the vector coverage in the correct order (oldest on the bottom, most recent on the top), converting the shapefile to a raster and subtracting the result from the year for which FRID is to be calculated (in this case the last year of the simulation).

FRID is calculated by dividing the "last burned" raster by the FRI raster (see "Fire Return Intervals" under the "Optional Data" section above). The process should be repeated for both the hypothetical atlas and the realized fire atlas to facilitate comparisons between the FRID of the hypothetical landscape (Fig. 16) and the FRID of the realized landscape (Fig. 17). In the case study, the FRID of realized landscape was subtracted from the FRID of the hypothetical landscape, resulting in a map showing the difference in FRID between the two alternative landscapes (Fig. 18).

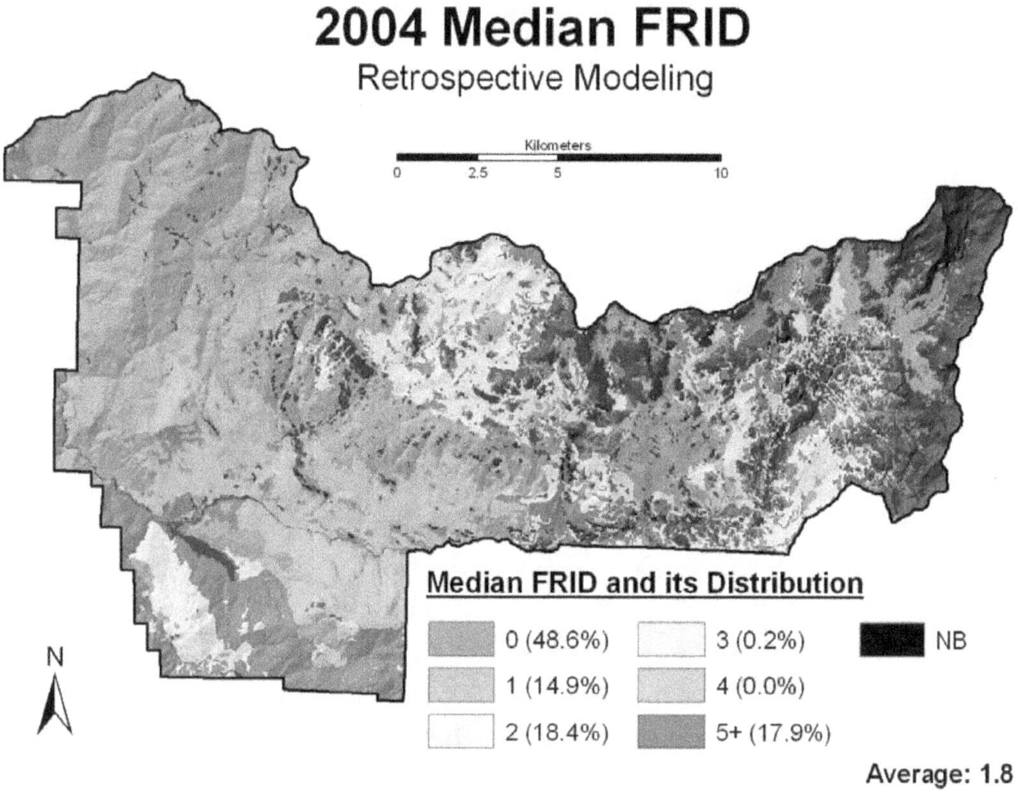

2004 Median FRID

Retrospective Modeling

Figure 16. FRID resulting from the alternative fire management strategy.

Median FRID and its Distribution

0 (48.6%)	3 (0.2%)	NB
1 (14.9%)	4 (0.0%)	
2 (18.4%)	5+ (17.9%)	

Average: 1.8

2004 Median FRID

No Retrospective Modeling

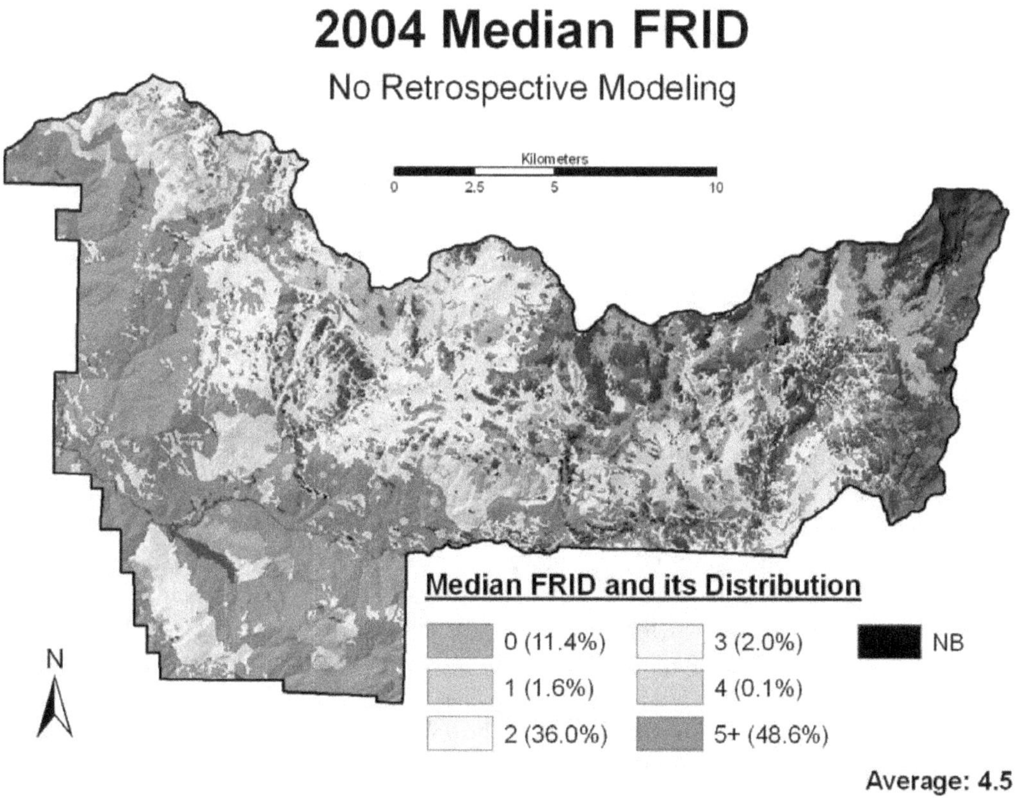

Figure 17. FRID resulting from the actual fire management strategy.

Median FRID and its Distribution

0 (11.4%)	3 (2.0%)	NB
1 (1.6%)	4 (0.1%)	
2 (36.0%)	5+ (48.6%)	

Average: 4.5

Difference in 2004 Median FRID

Retrospective Modeling vs Actual

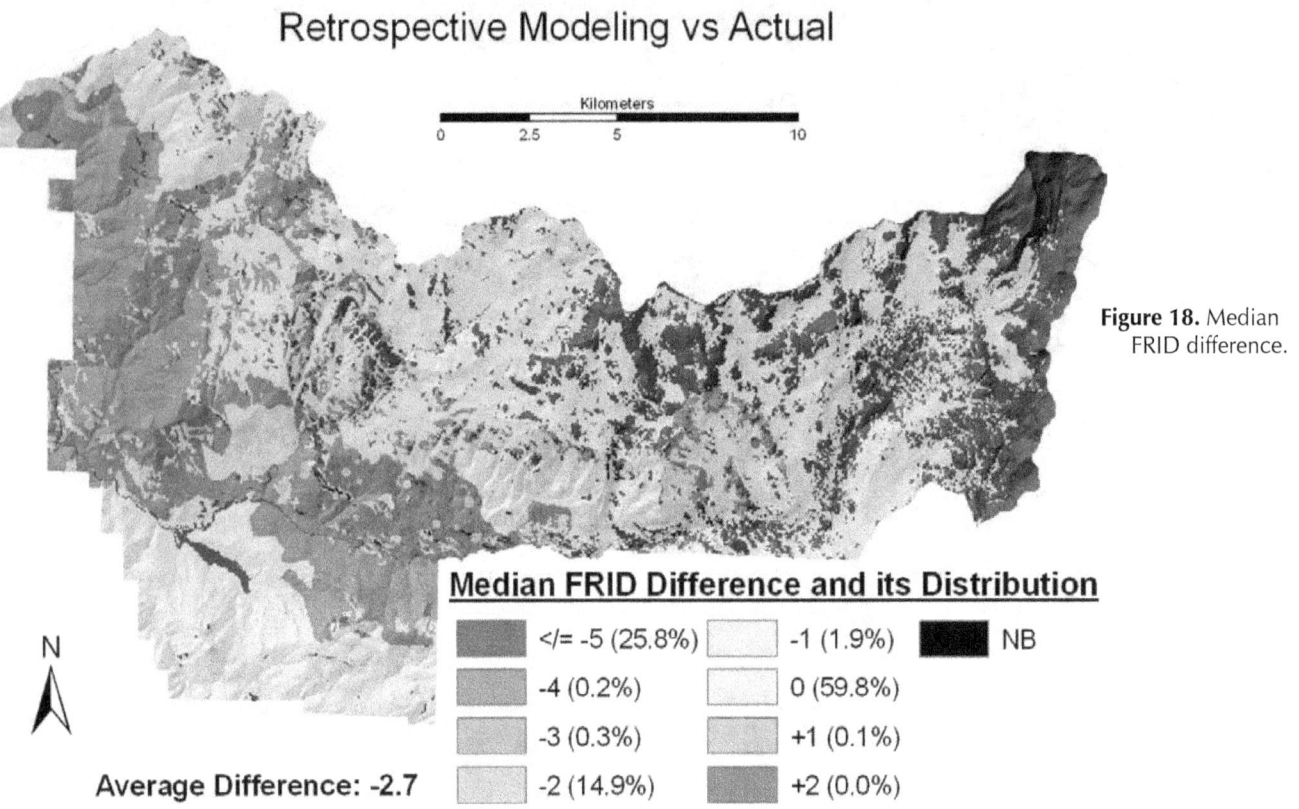

Figure 18. Median FRID difference.

Median FRID Difference and its Distribution

</= -5 (25.8%)	-1 (1.9%)	NB
-4 (0.2%)	0 (59.8%)	
-3 (0.3%)	+1 (0.1%)	
-2 (14.9%)	+2 (0.0%)	

Average Difference: -2.7

N

Potential Fire Behavior

Similar to the FRID analysis, the impact of suppression on potential fire behavior can be quantified by comparing the hypothetical and realized landscapes. For the case study, flame length was calculated for both landscapes using FlamMap. As outlined previously, FlamMap uses a LCP file, as does FARSITE, and requires fuel moisture, wind speed, and wind direction inputs. For the case study, fuel moistures and wind are held constant, and FlamMap calculates potential fire behavior for each location on the landscape for these static conditions. These predictions are static in that they are made without respect to fire spread across the landscape or changes in fuel moistures or wind. FlamMap should run by someone with experience with the software. The FlamMap tutorial can be used to gain familiarity with its configuration, assumptions, and limitations.

FlamMap inputs: The analyst will need two LCP files to compare the two alternative landscapes. Also required are wind speed and direction and fuel moisture files. It is common to use wind and fuel moisture values that reflect the upper percentiles of fire behavior indices such as ERC or SC to accentuate FlamMap outputs. Fuel moisture and wind data can be calculated for particular fire weather index percentiles using FFP. In the case study, the fuel moisture values (.fms file) were calculated based on the 98th percentile ERC; the wind values were based on 98th percentile wind speed and the most common wind direction observed during the fire season was also used. The 98th percentile ERC and the 98th percentile wind speed will rarely co-occur and in this case study, were arbitrarily selected.

For the hypothetical landscape, the final retrospective fire modeling LCP file was used. This file incorporated fuel succession after the last year of fire simulation. For the realized landscape, the fuel succession model was run for the same years as the modeled landscape using only "real" fire severities. Canopy fuels for the realized landscape were updated in the same manner as described in the "Canopy fuels updates" section above.

Running FlamMap: Repeat the following steps for both the hypothetical and realized landscapes: Load the LCP file (Theme > FARSITE Landscape File) into FlamMap. Set up a new run, import the fuel moisture file and set the wind speed and direction (azimuth) (Fig. 19). Import a custom fuel model file if necessary. Select the desired fire behavior outputs ("Fire Behavior Outputs" tab of the run window). Verify the units for each output (Options > Preferences > Edit Preferences). Run the program after the inputs and outputs are set. When the run is complete, save the results. These should be saved as GRID ASCII files for input into a GIS. Loading them into a GIS allows for further analysis (e.g., differencing the two scenarios) and the creation of maps illustrating analysis results (Figs. 20 and 21).

Figure 19. FlamMap inputs.

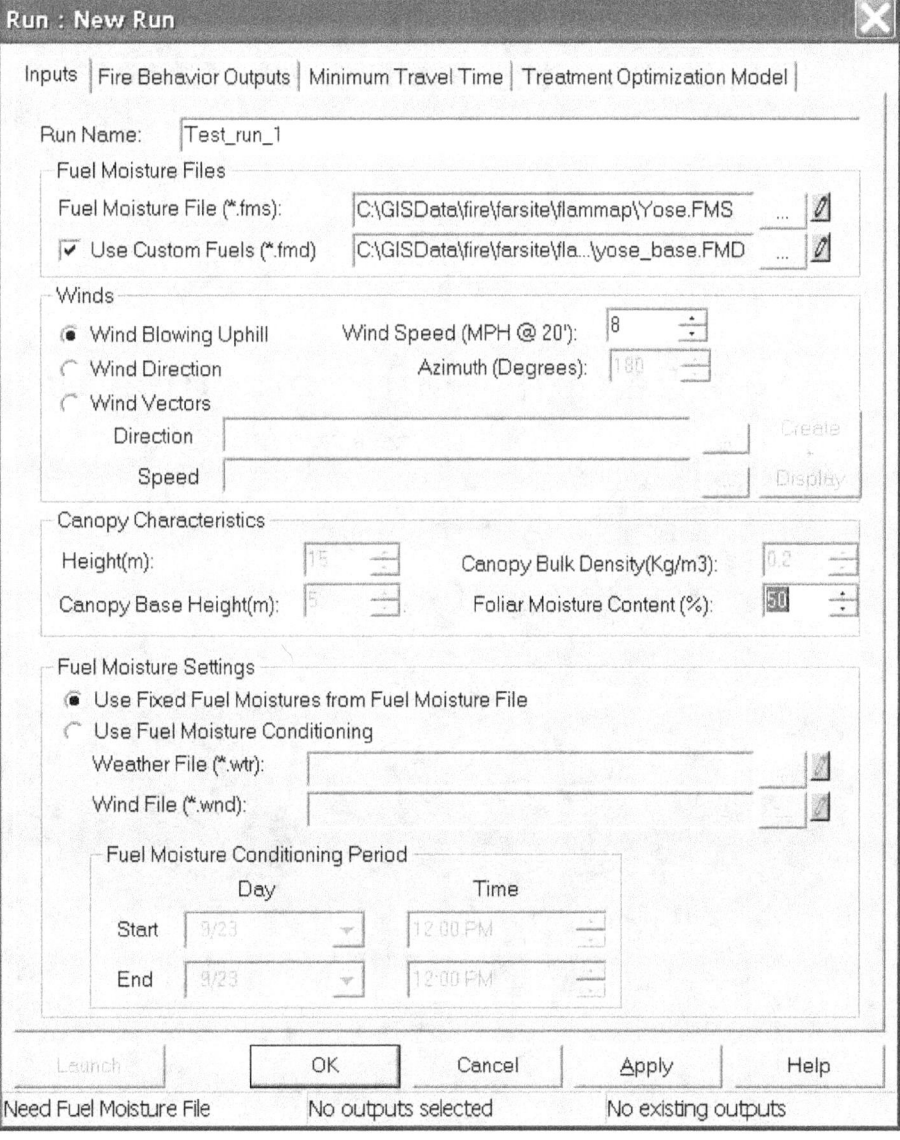

Flame Length - 98th Percentile Weather

No Retrospective Modeling

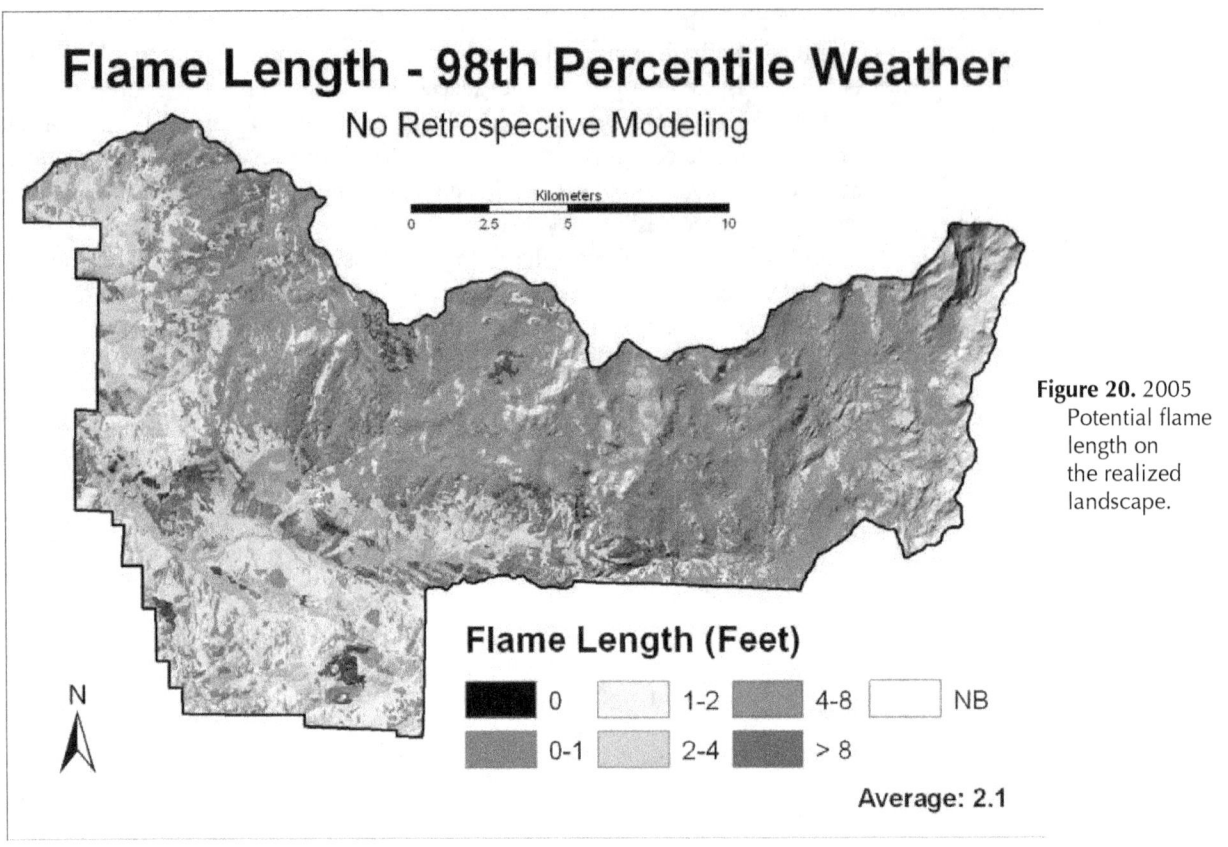

Figure 20. 2005 Potential flame length on the realized landscape.

Flame Length (Feet)

■ 0	☐ 1-2	▨ 4-8	☐ NB
▨ 0-1	☐ 2-4	■ > 8	

Average: 2.1

N

Flame Length - 98th Percentile Weather

Post Retrospective Modeling

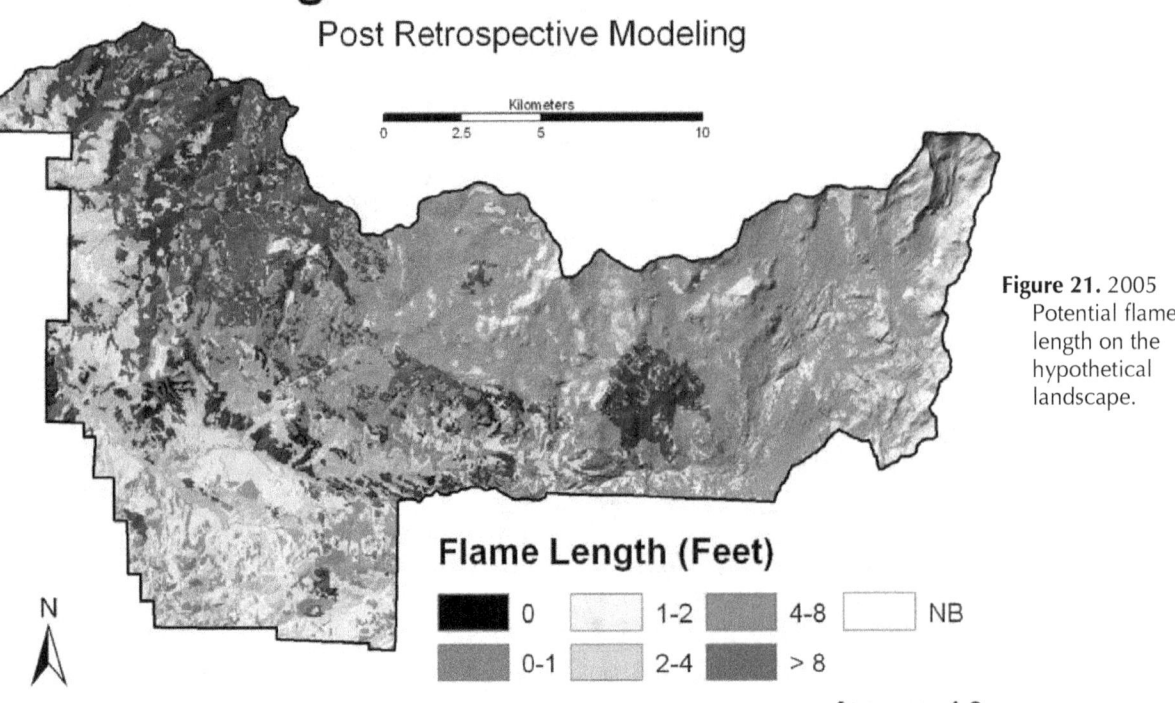

Figure 21. 2005 Potential flame length on the hypothetical landscape.

Flame Length (Feet)

■ 0	☐ 1-2	■ 4-8	☐ NB
■ 0-1	☐ 2-4	■ > 8	

Average: 1.3

N

Potential Smoke Emissions

The concept of potential emissions was described in the "Model Selection" section above. In this case study, potential PM 2.5 and PM 10 emissions were calculated using the Emission Estimation System (EES) for both the hypothetical and realized landscapes. In addition, the fuel succession model was run from the end year of the simulation analysis, 2004, through 2015 (assuming no fires after the end of the simulation in 2004) to see how potential emissions might rebound over time as fuel accumulation and post-fire fuel recovery occur (Figs. 22 and 23). For the case study smoke emissions were analyzed beyond 2004 to estimate the time period during which the landscape would have reduced potential emissions due to the hypothetical fire management strategies.

YOSE Potential PM 2.5 Emissions (EES)

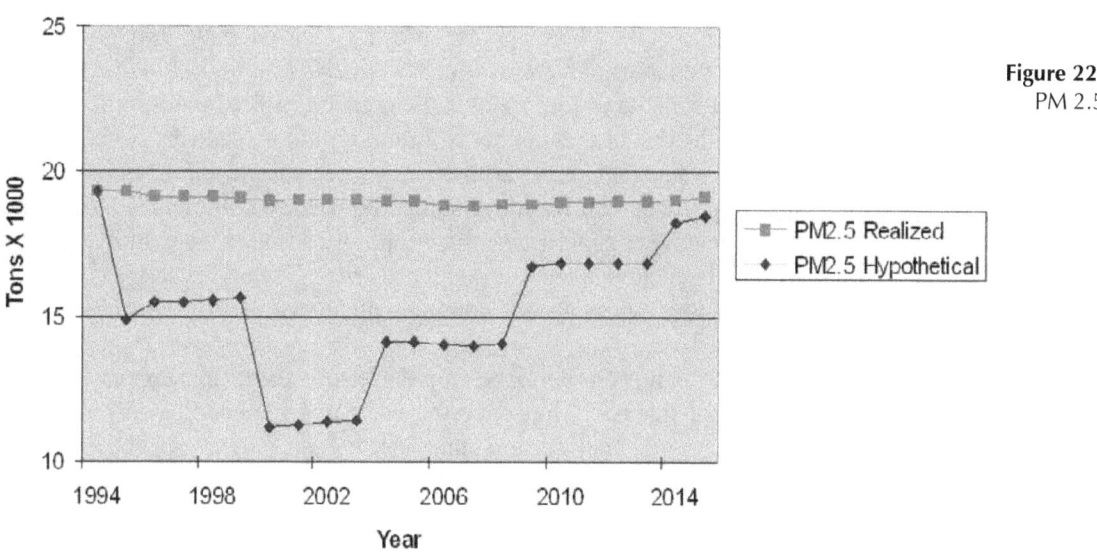

Figure 22. Potential PM 2.5 emissions.

YOSE Potential PM 10 Emissions (EES)

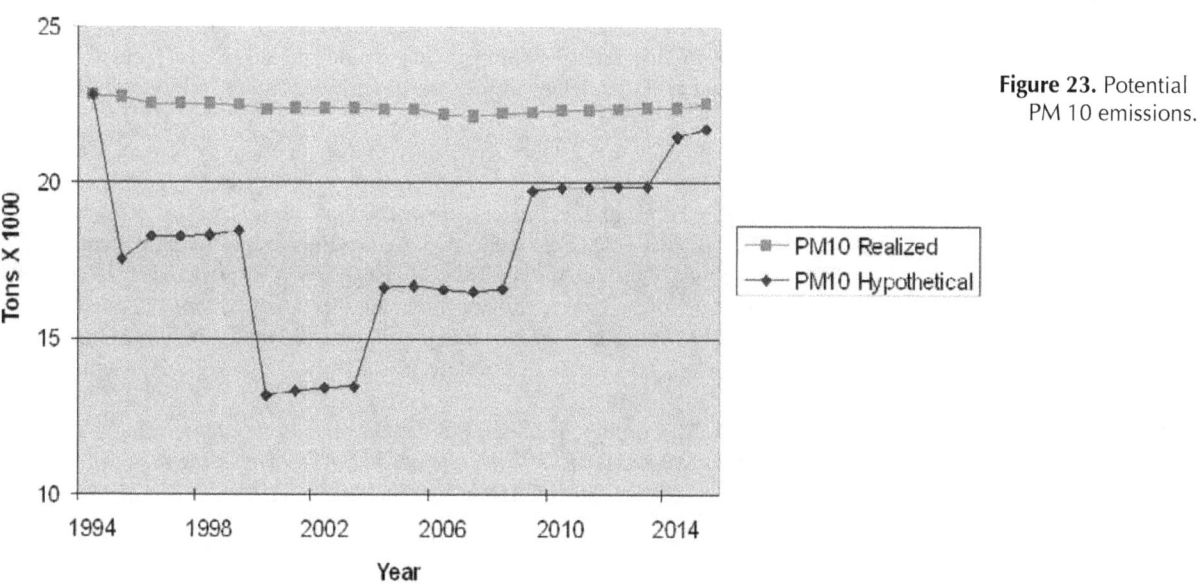

Figure 23. Potential PM 10 emissions.

Summary

The suppression of naturally occurring wildfires has an untold impact on fire dependent landscapes. The ability to quantify the impact of wildfire suppression can provide valuable insight to land managers. While the decision to allow an ignition to burn provides immediate feedback to land managers, in terms of fire behavior and effects, the impacts of the decision to suppress an ignition are not as immediate or clear.

This guidebook demonstrates a methodology to measure suppression impacts. The information developed through the retrospective fire modeling methodology can help managers make more informed decisions on whether to suppress an ignition. Retrospective fire modeling can be used to track the cumulative effects of fire suppression on indicators of the ecological health such as FRID or FRCC. It can also provide a means to compare the potential behavior of future fires. Simulating where suppressed ignitions might have spread can help managers prioritize future fuel treatments. For example, treatment preference might be given to areas where opportunities for fuel reduction through fire use have been foregone due to suppression. The analysis can reveal the managerial and ecological benefits of fire, such as the creation of fire breaks, reduction of fuel loadings, decline in the number of future ignitions requiring initial attack, improvement in fire regime departures, and a decrease in the potential severity of future fire behavior. Results can also be used to communicate tradeoffs inherent in allowing or suppressing fire on the landscape to the public and other governmental agencies such as air quality districts. The ability to measure suppression impacts provides a more complete picture of the consequences of the "go/no go" decision.

Using these methods to track the cumulative effects of fire suppression may initially be time intensive, but once the tools and methodologies have been chosen and the initial analyses are complete, it can easily be appended for future fires/ignitions and quickly updated on an annual basis. We believe that the advantages of the insights gained far outweigh the initial development costs. Happy modeling!

References

Albini, F.A. 1976. Estimating wildfire behavior and effects. Gen. Tech. Rep. INT-GTR-30. Ogden, UT: U.S. Department of Agriculture, Forest Service, Intermountain Forest and Range Experiment Station. 92 p.

Albini, F.A. 1979. Spot fire distance from burning trees: a predictive model. Gen. Tech. Rep. INT-GTR-56. Ogden, UT: U.S. Department of Agriculture, Forest Service, Intermountain Forest and Range Experiment Station. 73 p.

Andrews, P.L.; Bevins, C.D.; Seli, R.C. 2005. BehavePlus fire modeling system, version 3.0: user's guide. Gen. Tech. Rep. RMRS-GTR-106WWW. Ogden, UT: Department of Agriculture, Forest Service, Rocky Mountain Research Station. 142 p.

Box, G.E.P. 1979. Robustness in the strategy of scientific model building. In: Launer, R.L.; Wilkinson, G.N., eds. Robustness in statistics. New York: Academic Press: 201-235.

Bradshaw, L.S.; McCormick, E. 2000. FireFamily plus user's guide, version 2.0. Gen. Tech. Rep. RMRS-GTR-67WWW. Ogden, UT: U.S. Department of Agriculture, Forest Service, Rocky Mountain Research Station.

Brown, T.J.; Hall, B.L.; Mohrle, C.R.; Reinbold, H.J. 2002. Coarse assessment of Federal wildland fire occurrence data. CEFA Rep. 02-04. [Online]. Available: www. cefa.dri.edu/Publications.

Caprio, A.; Conover, C.; Keifer, M.; Lineback, P. 2002. Fire management and GIS: a framework for identifying and prioritizing fire planning needs. In: Sugihara, Neil G.; Morales, Maria; Morales, Tony, eds. Fire in California ecosystems: integrating ecology, prevention and management: Proceedings of the symposium; 1997 November 17-20; San Diego, CA. Misc. Pub. No. 1. Association for Fire Ecology: 102-113.

Caprio, Anthony C.; Lineback, Pat. 2002. Pre-twentieth century fire history of Sequoia and Kings Canyon National Park: a review and evaluation of our knowledge. In: Sugihara, Neil G.; Morales, Maria; Morales, Tony, eds. Fire in California ecosystems: integrating ecology, prevention and management: Proceedings of the symposium; 1997 November 17-20; San Diego, CA. Misc. Pub. No. 1. Association for Fire Ecology: 180-199.

Clinton, N.; Pu, R.; Gong, P.; Tian, Y.; Scarborough, J. 2003. Extension and input refinement to the ARB wildland fire emissions estimation model. Final report. ARB contract number 00-729. Berkley, CA: Center for the Assessment and Monitoring of Forest and Environmental Resources, College of Natural Resources, University of California. [Online]. Available: http://www.arb.ca.gov/research/apr/past/00-729.pdf [September 30, 2009].

Davis, B.H.; van Wagtendonk, J.W.; Beck, J.; van Wagtendonk, K. 2009. Modeling fuel succession. Fire Management Today. 69(2): 18-21.

Environmental Systems Research Institute [ESRI]. 2005. ArcGIS. Version 9.1. ESRI, Redlands, CA.

Finney, M.A. 1998. FARSITE: fire area simulator—model development and evaluation. Res. Pap. RMRS-RP-4. Ogden, UT: U.S. Department of Agriculture, Forest Service, Rocky Mountain Research Station. 47 p.

Finney, M.A. 2006. An overview of FlamMap modeling capabilities. In: Andrews, Patricia L.; Butler, Bret W., comps. Fuels management—how to measure success: conference proceedings; 2006 March 28-30; Portland, OR. Proc. RMRS-P-41. Fort Collins, CO: U.S. Department of Agriculture, Forest Service, Rocky Mountain Research Station. 809 p.

Heinsch, F.A.; Andrews, P.L.; Kurth, L.L. 2009. Implications of using percentiles to define fire danger levels. Extended Abstract P1.5. In: Eighth Symposium on Fire and Forest Meteorology, 12-15 October, 2009, Kalispell, MT>

Key, C.H.; Benson, N.C. 2006. Landscape assessment: remote sensing of severity, the normalized burn ratio. In: Lutes, D.C.; Keane, R.E.; Caratti, J.F.; Key, C.H.; Benson, N.C.; Sutherland, S.; Gangi, L.J., eds. FIREMON: fire effects monitoring and inventory system. Gen. Tech. Rep. RMRS-GTR-164-CD. Fort Collins, CO: U.S. Department of Agriculture, Forest Service, Rocky Mountain Research Station. 1 CD.

Landres, P.B.; Morgan, P.; Swanson, F.J. 1999. Overview of the use of natural variability concepts in managing ecological systems. Ecological Applications. 9(4): 1179-88.

National Interagency Fire Center. 2006. Interagency standards for fire and aviation operations. NFES 2724. Boise, ID. [Online]. Available: http://www.nifc.gov/policies/red_book/2006 htm.

Nelson, R.M., Jr. 2000. Prediction of diurnal change in 10-h fuel stick moisture content. Canadian Journal of Forest Research. 30: 1071-1087.

Reinhardt, E.D.; Crookston, N.L. 2003. The fire and fuels extension to the forest vegetation simulator. Gen. Tech. Rep. RMRS-GTR-116. Ogden, UT: U.S. Department of Agriculture, Forest Service, Rocky Mountain Research Station. 209 p.

Reinhardt, E.D.; Keane, R.E.; Brown, J.K. 1997. First order fire effects model: FOFEM 4.0, user's guide. Gen. Tech. Rep. INT-GTR-344. Ogden, UT: U.S. Department of Agriculture, Forest Service, Intermountain Research Station. 65 p.

Rollins, M.G. 2009. LANDFIRE: a nationally consistent vegetation, wildland fire, and fuel assessment. International Journal of Wildland Fire. 18(3): 235-249.

Rothermel, R.C. 1972. A mathematical model for predicting fire spread in wildland fuels. Res. Pap. INT-RP-115. Ogden, UT: U.S. Department of Agriculture, Forest Service, Intermountain Forest and Range Experiment Station. 40 p.

Rothermel, R.C. 1991. Predicting behavior and size of crown fires in the northern Rocky Mountains. Res. Pap. INT-RP-438. Ogden, UT: U.S. Department of Agriculture, Forest Service, Intermountain Forest and Range Experiment Station. 46 p.

Schmidt, K.M.; Menakis, J.P.; Hardy, C.C.; Hann, W.J.; Bunnell, D.L. 2002. Development of coarse-scale spatial data for wildland fire and fuel management. Gen. Tech. Rep. RMRS-GTR-87. Fort Collins, CO: U.S. Department of Agriculture, Forest Service, Rocky Mountain Research Station. 41 p. + CD.

Scott, J.H.; Burgan, R.E. 2005. Standard fire behavior fuel models: a comprehensive set for use with Rothermel's surface fire spread model. Gen. Tech. Rep. RMRS-GTR-153. Fort Collins, CO: U.S. Department of Agriculture, Forest Service, Rocky Mountain Research Station. 72 p.

Stratton, Richard D. 2006. Guidance on spatial wildland fire analysis: models, tools, and techniques. Gen. Tech. Rep. RMRS-GTR-183. Fort Collins, CO: U.S. Department of Agriculture, Forest Service, Rocky Mountain Research Station. 15 p.

Stratton, Richard D. 2009. Guidebook on LANDFIRE fuels data acquisition, critique, modification, maintenance, and model calibration. Gen. Tech. Rep. RMRS-GTR-220. Fort Collins, CO: U.S. Department of Agriculture, Forest Service, Rocky Mountain Research Station. 54 p.

Thode, A.E. 2005. Quantifying the fire regime attributes of severity and spatial complexity using field and imagery data. Davis, CA: University of California. Dissertation.

Tymstra, C.; Bryce, R.W.; Wotton, B.M.; Armitage, O.B. In press. Development and assessment of the Prometheus fire growth simulation model. Nat. Resour. Can., Can. For. Serv., North. For. Cent., Edmonton, AB. Inf. Rep. NOR-X-417. Forthcoming.

U.S. Department of Agriculture, Forest Service [USDAFS]. 2000. RERAP user's guide: version 5.03. Boise, ID: U.S. Department of Agriculture, Forest Service, National Fire and Aviation Management Information Systems Team. 154 p.

Van Wagner, C.E. 1977. Conditions for the start and spread of a crown fire. Canadian Journal of Forest Research. 71(3): 23-34.

Van Wagner, C.E. 1993. Prediction of crown fire behavior in two stands of jack pine. Canadian Journal of Forest Research: 23(3): 442-449.

Wiitala, M.R.; Carlton, D.W. 1994. Assessing long-term fire movement risk in wilderness fire management. In: Proceedings of the 12th conference on fire and forest meteorology; 1993 October 26-28; Jekyll Island, GA. Society of American Foresters: 187-194.